Architectural Policy in Finland
Architecture as civic education

jovis

Turit Fröbe

Architectural Policy in Finland

Architecture as civic education

jovis

9 Introduction

19 Baukultur in Finland and Germany
Structural and historical conditions
31 Baukultur in Finland and Germany—a subjective impression

45 Finnish architectural policy—a learning process
49 The specifics of Finland's Architectural Policy from 1998
56 Local and regional architectural policies
64 APOLI2020
69 Conclusion: Processes in architectural policy

75 Architecture as civic education
78 Archinfo Finland
85 Architecture competitions as civic education
93 Conclusion: Civic education in Baukultur

97 Architecture in the Finnish educational system
98 Architecture education in the regular school system
109 Architecture education in Basic Education in the Arts
117 Conclusion: Integrate Baukultur into the educational system!

125 Institutions in architecture education
Architecture education at university level
131 ARKKI, Lastu, and others
137 Recent trends in architecture education in Finland
147 Conclusion: Baukultur-Teaching, further education and training

153 Architectural policy programs as promoters of architecture education for children and youth in Finland
Jaana Räsänen (guest contributor)

163 Closing remarks
169 Recommendations

177 References
183 Image credits

I would like to thank my interlocutors, who frankly provided me with information, insights, and materials, for their support!

This publication would not have been possible without your help!

Introduction

For years, Finland has been considered a pioneer in all aspects of Baukultur policy and Baukultur education. In 1998, Finland was one of the first countries in Europe to adopt an official *Architectural Policy,* which is—until today—consulted internationally and has not only been translated into Swedish and English, but also into French, Spanish, German, and later Arabic.[1] A prominent part of this program was devoted to "architecture education" with the aim of improving the general education and public awareness of architecture. It was for this reason that, from 2001 onwards, the English term "civic education in architecture"[2] was sometimes used in Finland.

Civic education in architecture became necessary because in 1995 the right to a suitably designed and healthy environment was enshrined in the catalog of fundamental rights in the Finnish constitution and this right was also linked to civic obligations.[3] The Finnish constitution obliged the nation's populace to care for their cultural heritage and to participate in decision-making processes concerning their own living environment.[4] In order to enable citizens to fulfil these duties, it was necessary to provide society with architectural knowledge and a general education in Baukultur. With the *Architectural Policy* proclaimed in 1998, Baukultur education was declared a lifelong civic learning task. One of the declared goals was to anchor architecture education more systematically in the school system as well as in the curricula of teacher training programs. It was also agreed to integrate it into adult education and train politicians and decision-makers in the cities and municipalities.[5]

Soon enough, the first success stories emerged from Finland. The media and articles on Baukultur reported that architecture education had already been included in the *National core curricula* in 2003 and had thus become a fixed component of the programs in planning.[6] According to other sources, architecture education had already been a compulsory part of art lessons since 1993.[7] There have been reports from schools with an architectural focus[8] and from architecture schools for children and young people, such as ARKKI, the School of Architecture for Children and Youth in Helsinki, or the LASTU School in Lapinlahti, where since 1993 four-to-nineteen-year-olds have been taught in continuous classes, and where they can each be taught a staggering amount of up to 1,800 hours of lessons in architecture, provided that they continuously attend classes from early childhood until they graduate.[9] Coupled with the outstanding results that Finland achieved in the PISA studies carried out from 2000 onwards, which attested to the outstanding quality of the Finnish school system,[10] everything suddenly seemed possible—especially since Finland was also known for its traditionally exceptionally high proportion of art lessons in the school system.[11]

When it became public at the "Convention on Baukultur 2018" in Potsdam, organized by the Federal Foundation of Baukultur, that the German government was planning to adopt German *Guidelines for Baukultur* during its EU presidency in the second half of 2020, it was decided to conduct a field study in Finland at the Berlin University of the Arts. It focuses on the question of how successful the *Architectural Policy* of 1998 actually has been and what Germany can possibly learn from the Finnish experience for its own upcoming processes. Has it been possible to improve the general awareness of Baukultur in society? Were the Finns able to systematically anchor architecture education in the school and educational system? What is being taught, and how do these seminars prepare future teachers to teach Baukultur? Has it been possible to integrate architecture education into the teaching curricula at universities and introduce prospective teachers to architecture and urban planning in the course of their studies? How have advanced education programs been organized and structured and what teaching materials have been designed and are available? Above all, the question arose as to whether it is at all possible for Germany to learn and transfer experiences from a country like Finland, which has greatly different structural and historical preconditions.

During an eight-day stay in Helsinki, the field study involved discussions with representatives from a wide range of professions, which were later supplemented by Skype, telephone, or email interviews in order to include perspectives that range beyond the metropolitan area around Helsinki. In this way, it was possible to identify and address a number of misunderstandings about the Finnish educational system and the role of architecture education, which, however, did not change the overall assessment that Finland is still the undisputed pioneer in the field of architecture education.

Certainly the biggest surprise revealed by the study was the joyful news with which the author was greeted by Hanna Harris, Director of Archinfo Finland, immediately after her arrival in Helsinki on 6 May 2019: "Finland is getting a new architectural policy! The press release will be sent out today!" The official work was already supposed to start in the following week so that APOLI2020 could be completed in the Fall of 2020, she elaborated.[12] This announcement unexpectedly opened up new perspectives and questions. Why does Finland, which is famous for its *Architectural Policy*, need a revised version of the same? Which contents and topics will be relevant for the new process? How will it be organized? Who will be involved? At the same time, the announcement raised certain doubts. Does it even make any sense to want to learn from a 20-year-old process—at a time when the Finns begin to move towards a new edition with their *Architectural Policy*, characterizing the old one as "too old to be implemented" and "no longer relevant in the face of many social changes"?[13]

In the following, we will first take a look at the different historical and structural preconditions of the two countries and will strive to assess the situation of Baukultur in both countries.

In the second and partly also the third chapter, the *Architectural Policy* of 1998 and its two- or three-phase implementation process will be presented and evaluated. In addition, an insight into the current APOLI2020 processes will be given. For this purpose, the author of this study spoke to Hanna Harris, director of Archinfo Finland, and Petra Havu, who is a counsellor for cultural affairs in the Ministry of Education and Culture's Department of Arts and Cultural Policy, both of whom are playing a key role in the development of the new architectural policy. Of particular importance were the discussions and extensive correspondence with Tiina Valpola, the retired founding director of Archinfo Finland, who, as special advisor for architecture for the National Council for Architecture from 2004 to 2012, was instrumental in implementing the 1998 *Architectural Policy* and in this position also built up Archinfo Finland, which can justifiably be considered the greatest success of the Finnish *Architectural Policy*.

In chapter 3, which deals with the question of the extent to which general architecture education could be improved in Finnish society and what measures and strategies are being used to further this aim, the institution Archinfo Finland is introduced to show, for instance, how the Finnish competition system has been employed to enhance overall architectural awareness across society. Mari Koskinen, competition specialist in the Finnish Association of Architects SAFA, provided valuable information on this subject.

Chapter 4 focuses on the implementation of architecture education in the school and educational system. Discussions were held with Mikko Hartikainen from the Finnish National Agency for Education, Dr. Riikka Mäkikoskela, executive director of the Finnish Association of Art Schools for Children and Young People, and Henna Haavisto, teacher at the Aurinkolahti Primary School in Vuosaari. In this chapter, but especially in the following one, a number of protagonists in the field of Finnish architecture education were consulted, such as Pihla Meskanen, founder of ARKKI, School of Architecture for Children and Youth in Helsinki, and its newly appointed director, Jaana Räsänen, who worked as a specialist for architecture education at Archinfo Finland until April 2019, Mervi Eskelinen, founder of the Lastu School of Architecture and Environmental Culture in Lapinlathi, Ilpo Vuorela from the Jyväskylä Adult Education Centre, and Else Luotinen and Ruud Ronni from the newly founded Tiili School of Architecture in Tampere.

The last chapter centers on the institutions and actors in architecture education, some of whom have already been mentioned. In addition, the role of universities in relation to architecture education is considered, with Professor Martti Raevaara, head of the Master's program in Art Education and of the Faculty of Arts at the Aalto University School of Arts, Design and Architecture, who kindly provided insight into how prospective art teachers undergo preparation to teach children and young people about architecture and urban planning. Finally, the mediation work at the two major Finnish architecture museums is presented. Arja-Liisa Kaasinen, head of collaboration and engagement, provided information on how mediation is organized at the Museum of Finnish Architecture, and Lotta Leskelä, curator of education at the Alvar Aalto Museum in Jyväskylä, reported on new strategies in her institute.

In a guest contribution, Jaana Räsänen describes the extent to which local and regional architectural policies, which emerged as a result of the 1998 national architectural policy program, have become promoters of architecture education.

Chapters 2 to 5 are organized in such a way that each chapter ends with a brief summary highlighting the situation in Germany. At the end of the publication, concrete recommendations are made for the development process of the German *Guidelines for Baukultur.*

It should be made clear at this point that a number of Finnish institutions and authorities have changed their names over the past 20 years, which can tend to be confusing:

+ In 2010, the Ministry of Education and the Ministry of Culture were fused into a dual ministry, the Ministry of Education and Culture,
+ The National Board of Education became the Finnish National Agency for Education,
+ The Arts Council of Finland has been known as Arts Promotion Centre Finland since 2013, and
+ The National Council for Architecture was renamed the National Council for Architecture and Design.

In the following text, these entities bear the titles by which they were known at the time and, where necessary, a note drawing attention to this has been added. Furthermore, the author of this study decided to adopt the different designations common in both countries. In the Finnish context, for example, the terms “architecture education” and “architectural policy” are used, while in Germany the most commonly used related terms are “Baukultur education” and “Baukultur policy.”

1 Cf. http://archinfo.fi/2014/01/valtioneuvoston-arkkitehtuuripoliittinen-ohjelma-1998/ (accessed December 15, 2019).

2 Cf. Korpelainen and Yanar 2001.

3 Cf. The Constitution of Finland, 11 June 1999, Chapter 1 – Fundamental provisions § 20 – Responsibility for the environment: "Nature and its biodiversity, the environment and the national heritage are the responsibility of everyone. The public authorities shall endeavor to guarantee for everyone the right to a healthy environment and for everyone the possibility to influence the decisions that concern their own living environment." Cf. https://www.finlex.fi/fi/laki/kaannokset/1999/de19990731.pdf (last accessed January 19, 2020).

4 Cf. Architectural Policy 1999, p. 6, p. 15.

5 Cf. Architectural Policy 1999, pp. 15–17.

6 Cf. Feller 2005, p. 50.

7 Cf. Kataikko 2006, p. 39.

8 Cf. Kataikko 2006, p. 37.

9 Cf. Kataikko 2006, pp. 37–38, or cf. Feller, 2009, p. 51.

10 Cf. https://www.pisa.tum.de/fileadmin/w00bgi/www/Berichtsbaende_und_Zusammenfassungungen/Zusammenfassung_PISA_2000 (accessed January 10, 2020)

11 Cf. Busnach 2017.

12 Hanna Harris in conversation with the author, May 6, 2019 and cf. https://minedu.fi/artikkeli/-/asset_publisher/tyoryhma-laatimaan-arkkitehtuuripoliittista-ohjelmaa (accessed January 10, 2020).

13 Petra Havu in conversation with the author, May 6, 2019.

Baukultur in Finland and Germany

Structural and historical conditions

Is it at all possible to compare Finland and Germany with regard to their relationship to Baukultur or to derive recommendations from one country for the other? Or are the starting conditions ultimately so different that Germany could—eventually and with huge efforts—at best succeed in achieving a status quo that Finland already enjoyed before the creation of its *Architectural Policy* in 1998? Without doubt, the structural and historical starting conditions could hardly be more different. The small, centrally governed Finnish state with only 5.5 million inhabitants is juxtaposed with Germany's complex federal system that guarantees the federal states cultural sovereignty, including in the area of education. The basic conditions also differ historically.

Finland has a strong affinity with architecture, as this is closely linked to the nation-building process of the young state, which only declared its independence in 1917. In particular, it is thanks to the two protagonists Eliel Saarinen

Fig. 1

are the National Museum (1905–1919), built and designed together with Herman Gesellius and Armas Lindgren, and the Helsinki Central Railway Station (1904–1919). The latter, with its monumental pairs of lamp-bearing statues by Emil Wikström, became one of Helsinki's most important landmarks.[2] (Fig. 1) Saarinen achieved world fame at the end of the 1920s with his contribution to the Tribune Tower competition in Chicago, a renown similar to that of Alvar Aalto, now considered the father of so-called Scandinavian design. Aalto, who is revered as a national hero in Finland, turned to a kind of "naturalization" of New Building after a brief functionalist phase in the mid-1930s. He began to interweave local materials and building traditions and adopted an organic formal language with that of New Building.[3] According to Asko Salokorpi, his "local variation of international architecture" was "perceived as just as national as Saarinen's national romantic architecture."[4] Hence, both architects contributed significantly to the formation of a Finnish identity and self-confidence. In conversation, Arja-Liisa Kaasinen of the Museum of Finnish Architecture noted that it is warrantable to say that the nation was built by architects. As an upshot of this, interest in architecture and architectural history is still well anchored in today's society.[5] According to Riikka Mäkikoskela, this pronounced awareness of architecture is also due to the fact that "the Finns traditionally built their houses with their own hands. So, they are familiar with architecture, building, and craft. When you get married and start a family in Finland, you usually build a house for your family."[6]

The societal starting conditions for architecture in Germany are quite different. With reference to the passionately conducted debates in the press, Germans are often described as taking a fundamental interest in Baukultur. However, these media debates usually refer to outstanding forms of spectacle architecture, reconstructions, or building scandals. Generally, the public holds a rather "limited concept of architecture," with the result that "buildings of daily use are not even perceived from an architectural point of view."[7] Accordingly, the vast majority of citizens regard architecture and urban planning as specialized disciplines that have little or nothing to do with their own lived reality.

The fact that Germans have a relatively distanced relationship to their Baukultur is also perhaps partly due to historical factors. In large parts of the country, the issue of Baukultur is linked to the experience of loss. During the Second World War, many cities lost large swathes of their old structures and were hastily rebuilt in line with a more or less modern model. Just how present this trauma of loss still is today can be seen in the debates around reconstruction throughout the country. In many places, the better-not-look-too-closely paradigm was already inscribed in the cityscape during reconstruction, in that only the cityscape's key buildings were reconstructed, and everything in between was filled with relatively neutral functional architecture. In addition, there was also a political tendency in both the post-war and post-reunification periods to rely on an architecture of restraint for fear of signaling a false sense of self-confidence, as Peter Conradi puts it.[8] It is therefore fair to assume that, due to these reasons, the debate on Baukultur in the sense of a civic general education has not necessarily been promoted and promulgated in Germany for a long time. Furthermore, architectural and urban history in Germany appear incomparably more complex and less accessible than in Finland, which certainly also contributes to the fact that Baukultur is generally regarded as a specialist discipline. While Finnish architectural history is essentially a history of modernism—which is not only due to the nation's relatively recent independence but also to the historically predominant tradition of timber construction that has only a relatively short life span—in Germany it is modernism in particular that the majority of citizens would like to see undone.

According to estimates by the Finnish National Board of Antiquities, only 20% of the country's buildings were built before 1955,[9] of which only a small percentage can be traced to Swedish architecture consisting of stone remains, such as castles, fortresses, and churches. Most cities in Germany, on the other hand,—depending on whether they originated from medieval foundations or Roman colonies—can look back on one or two millennia of an urban and architectural history characterized by vast regional diversity. This may explain why a broad overview of German Baukultur is more difficult to achieve than of the Finnish one. But does it also explain why the improvement of general architectural awareness in Germany has till now barely been promoted or demanded?

Today, a solid groundwork has been laid for improving public architectural awareness in Germany. Like Finland, Germany can look back on almost 20 years of national Baukultur policy, which has led to a remarkable institutionalization in recent years. Foundations, networks, and initiatives have been established not only at the federal and state level but also in many cities and municipalities, which have promoted Baukultur at the political level. The fact that it has nevertheless hardly been possible to anchor Baukultur more strongly in the social consciousness is due to a variety of reasons. For example, it rarely succeeds in addressing new target groups, as there are too few low-threshold provisions through which citizens can be introduced to architecture.[10] In addition, the institutions of Baukultur often still start from a rather narrowly defined normative concept of Baukultur and usually focus on "good building," "good design," or "important monuments." This creates unnecessary hurdles because it always assumes prior knowledge. However, this is primarily because—unlike in Finland where civic education in architecture has been at the center of the *Architectural Policy*—no corresponding goal or even need has ever been formulated in Germany. The topic of Baukultur education has only been put on the political agenda relatively recently. It was not until December 2017 that the Network for Baukultur Education was founded under the auspices of the Federal Foundation of Baukultur,[11] and it is only since March 2019 that this body has had a project staff member for this area. In addition, it has not yet been possible to systematically integrate Baukultur education into the educational system, although the conditions in Germany would appear to be promising. Architecture has already found its way into the framework curriculum for the subject of art across the states and at all school levels. However, since it has not yet been integrated into teacher training courses at universities, it currently depends on the individual interest of teachers whether pupils come into contact with architecture and Baukultur. When carried out in the school context, it is usually undertaken more or less voluntarily in the context of afternoon workshops and project weeks and implemented by external experts from the chambers of architects or the offices and associations for the protection of historical monuments. Particular mention should be made of the "Architektur macht Schule" program, which the federal chambers of architects now offer almost everywhere. However, since very few mediators are pedagogically trained, not all concepts are considered successful. It is noticeable that most projects are based on handicrafts, building, and

Fig. 2

Fig. 3

construction and are only rarely linked to Baukultur content and learning objectives.[12]

It is further remarkable that the broader terms "Baukultur policy" and "Baukultur education" have become established in Germany, while the focus is still comparatively narrow. Conversely—and this should be emphasized here—the much narrower terms "architectural policy" and "architecture education" are used in Finland, while the focus in terms of content is much broader than the terminology would suggest.

Overall, it can be assumed that the conditions for bringing architecture into public consciousness are certainly somewhat better in Finland than in Germany. However, the fact that basic attitudes do not greatly differ is shown by the rankings produced when a readers' poll is launched in the press to nominate the ugliest building in the city or country. It seems almost reassuring that in Finland, just as in Germany, the lists often feature important works of post-war architectural history with a secure place in architectural guides. Tiina Valpola, the retired founding director of Archinfo Finland, and Arja-Liisa Kaasinen of the Museum of Finnish Architecture have pointed out that a work by the national hero Alvar Aalto usually occupies one of the top places in these Finnish rankings.[13] The so-called "Sokeripala" (Sugar Cube; Fig. 2), as the Enso Gutzeit company headquarters built in 1962 is called, stands next to the Russian Orthodox Cathedral opposite the Presidential Palace and visually closes off the front of Kauppatori Market Square in Helsinki's southern harbor. Even its Finnish Wikipedia article presents it as "Finland's most hated building."[14] As Gareth Griffiths describes in his 1997 publication *The Polemical Aalto*, the office building was never uncontroversial, which is also—but not only—due to the fact that one of the so-called castles

Fig. 4

Fig. 5

typical of the Katajanokka district, the Norrmén House from 1907, was demolished to build it.[15] The national hero Alvar Aalto—who is much more than a star architect to the Finns—not only built Finlandia Hall (1971) (Fig. 3), Helsinki's landmark, but according to public opinion is also able to serve the lowest end of the architectural value scale. This testifies to a rather relaxed relationship between the Finns and their national hero Alvar Aalto.

Baukultur in Finland and Germany—a subjective impression

The architectural appearance of the cityscape ultimately shows that architecture and Baukultur play a different role and have a different status in Finland compared to Germany. Even if a number of mediators have sometimes been extremely critical of the quality of everyday Finnish architecture, the general standard appears high compared to that of Germany. Not only the public buildings but also the anonymous everyday architecture in Helsinki's metropolitan area appears to be of a higher and more ambitious quality than in Germany—this applies both to the post-war era and to contemporary architecture. Of course, Helsinki's cityscape also features sometimes less successful or more banal investor architecture, but this is considerably less widespread than in Germany. The chances of encountering well-designed details in an urban context—such as the lifeguard tower on the beach at Aurinkolahti in Vuosaari (Fig. 4)—is much higher than in Germany. What is striking is that Finnish architects are consistently committed to a modern style. The kinds of "historicisms" and "retro-architectures" that are currently booming in German investor architecture (Fig. 5) hardly play a role.[16]

Fig. 6

Fig. 7

Fig. 8

Fig. 9

Even more striking is the difference in the quality of public buildings. A glance at Helsinki's most recent architectural highlights alone— the new main building of Aalto University by Verstas, which opened in 2018 and is called the Väre Building, or the spectacular transformations or extensions by JKMM Architects—are striking evidence of an innovative approach to existing buildings and even architectural icons. After expanding Alvar Aalto's library on the Otaniemi Campus of Aalto University in 2016 to include the Harald Herlin Learning Centre and transforming a post-war administrative building at the University of Helsinki into the Think Corner in 2017, JKMM caused a sensation in 2018 with the Amos Rex art museum. With Amos Rex, the young office has succeeded in giving an underground extension to one of Helsinki's most important functionalist buildings, the "Lasipalatsi" (Glass Palace; Fig. 6), built in 1935/36. With its five dome-shaped roof constructions with skylights the extension appears in such a way that an inner-city wasteland that could not be built on was not only revitalized but also transformed into one of Helsinki's most popular public spaces, inviting a wide variety of uses. (Fig. 7) Architecture of high quality and innovation is of course also found in Germany, as the example of the Elbphilharmonie in Hamburg by Herzog & de Meuron shows, but these instances are comparatively rare.

What the above-mentioned examples of contemporary Finnish architecture have in common is that they create public or semi-public spaces and meeting zones, which—due to Finland's climate with its long, cold, and above all dark winters—seems to be more important than in German Baukultur. A radical redefinition of what public space can be has been achieved in Helsinki's most recent architectural icon, the Central Library Oodi by ALA Architects, (Fig. 8) which

Fig. 10

opened in December 2018. The programmatic character of the new building, which was planned as one of the key projects on the occasion of the 100th anniversary of Finnish independence, is already evident from its siting in Helsinki's cultural district.[17] It sits vis à vis the Parliament, in the immediate vicinity of Stephen Hall's Kiasma Museum of Contemporary Art, completed in 1998, and Alvar Aalto's Finlandia Hall, one of the landmarks of Helsinki, opened in 1971. Oodi is not only an ode, as its name implies, to books and reading but, as Helsinki's executive director of culture and leisure, Tommi Laitio, said at the opening ceremony: "It is also a symbol of the goals we have as a society."[18] Beate Detlefs asserts that a Finnish library is quite predestined to become such a meaningful symbol. She explains why libraries embody the quintessence of Finnish values—social encounter, sharing of resources, and community spirit—and notes that the library system is consistently integrated into the country's national educational and cultural strategies and thus assumes a different status in society. This is also reflected in the state funding sums, which in 2009 were 8.21 euros per capita per year in Germany and 54.55 euros in Finland.[19] Indeed, Oodi is setting new standards, exemplifying what a library can achieve in contemporary and future society. The concept emerged from a participatory process in 2012, in which citizens were asked both online and in workshops about their "dreams" for a library of the future and which became an important facet of the planning process.[20]

The actual library—the reading room with 100,000 books and generous reading, play, and recreation zones—is located in the so-called "Book Heaven,"[21] (Fig. 9) the fully glazed second floor. It overlooks Helsinki's cultural center and is enclosed by a gently curved, moving roof construction with organically shaped skylights. While the ground floor area houses a café-restaurant, cinema, auditorium, and the entire service area, the first floor in the closed belly of the building accommodates the new, future-oriented library functions. In the so-called Maker Space or "urban workshop", users are provided with state-of-the-art technology ranging from 3D printers, plotters, computers with image processing and layout software to computer-controlled knitting machines, sewing machines including ironing boards—to name just a few—which they can use with their regular library card. Musical instruments and iPads can be borrowed, and rehearsal rooms, music studios, and game spaces are available to rent, as well as workrooms for smaller or larger teams, for a small fee. In addition, there are recreational areas that are open to everyone. Under the heading "Non-discrimination" in the Oodi principles—which are formulated on a blackboard on the first floor but also on the library's website—it says: “Everyone has the right to be in the library. Idle hanging around is allowed and even encouraged.” And finally, under “Comfort and well-being” it is stated: “Oodi is our common living room. Everyone should respect the comfort and well-being of others.”[22] Seen in this light, Oodi is not only an ode to books and reading but also an ode to community, democracy, and public space—a model that may be desirable for Germany, but it hardly seems conceivable at present. While the idea of combining a public library with a maker-lab is already being tested in various places in Europe and sporadically in Germany—one of the pioneers being the public library in Cologne, where a maker-lab was installed in 2013[23]—the concept of a public space or “living room” (Fig. 10) like Oodi is hardly imaginable. Although it will become increasingly important to create public spaces that allow everyone to participate and which are not linked to consumption, public space in Germany is still being systematically robbed of its residential qualities—from fear of the homeless or noisy youths—by either removing seats in squares, parks, or pedestrian zones, or making them so uncomfortable and unwelcoming that it is hard to stay there for long. The fact that an experiment like Oodi has been feasible in Finland is a result of the marked decline in homelessness over the past ten years due to the “Housing First” program launched in 2008. This program provides unconditional housing to every homeless person, allowing them a base from which to address their other problems.[24]

Nowhere is Finland’s architectural ambition, building culture, and self-confidence in this realm more evident than in a March 28, 2019 press release from the Finnish Ministry of Culture and Education. Here, the ministry announced that plans are underway for a “world-class” architecture and design museum, whereby the previously separate museums of architecture and design, which are located in close proximity to each other, are to be merged into a new building in Helsinki's southern harbor district.[25] The website of the future museum supports this ambitious claim by stating that "the most attractive museum in the world" will be created. The aim is "to build Europe's Museum of the Year, which Finns can be proud of and which attracts people [from] all around the world."[26]

Given the country's current strengths in architecture, this could indeed become a model for "world-class" architecture. Yet nowhere is the difference in the policy landscape and attitudes in Germany more evident than in the planning of the National Bauakademie in Berlin, which is intended as a center of excellence for architecture. In contrast to Helsinki, Berlin will most likely not dare to experiment but will rather, as a precaution, rely on an old and proven icon, namely Karl-Friedrich Schinkel's Bauakademie, built between 1832 and 1836, which was severely damaged in the Second World War and torn down by the East German government in 1962. Whether an actual reconstruction or a more or less free interpretation of this lost Berlin icon will be created has not yet been decided. However, both the budget resolution passed by the Bundestag, in which 62 million euros were made available, and the program competition, which was decided in May 2018, ran under the conservative title "As much Schinkel as possible!"[27] (Fig. 11) Probably the biggest difference between the two plans in Helsinki and Berlin can be found in a sentence at the end of the March 28 press release, which stated that the city of Helsinki is prepared to support the construction of the new museum: "It is essential that the city invests in world-class content and experiences—not in walls only." In the case of the National Bauakademie in Berlin, however, investment will again be

(1873–1950) and Alvar Aalto (1898–1976) that Finland has traditionally seen itself as a nation of architecture and design. Both architects achieved international fame and made Finnish architecture a topos—with an equally important effect at home. Through their crucial contributions to the development of national architecture, both architects—and Aalto in particular—have played a major role in formulating Finnish identity.

As Seppo Zetterberg notes, a Finnish national movement only developed from 1809 onwards, when Finland—which had been under Swedish rule since the mid-13th century—became the political pawn of territorial struggles and was conquered by Russia in the Russian-Swedish war. Under Russian rule, Finland was granted the status of an autonomous grand duchy. In the course of the next 100 years, this enabled the Finns to establish their own state apparatus in the Russian Empire, with its own senate, judiciary, civil service, currency, national language, and eventually its own army. After Russia tried to contain Finnish separatism in two so-called phases of oppression at the beginning of the twentieth century, Finland finally took advantage of the turmoil of the Russian Revolution in 1917 to declare its independence.[1]

As early as 1812, the capital had been moved from Turku to Helsinki and under the German architect Carl Ludwig Engel had been developed into a classicist center. This helped the Finnish grand duchy to gain new self-confidence. According to Ritva Wäre, the search for an independent Finnish style in architecture began after 1890 and finally manifested itself particularly in the works of Saarinen and Aalto. At the beginning of the twentieth century, Saarinen combined traditional Finnish wooden architecture with elements of Art Nouveau and Historicism to create the so-called Finnish National Romanticism. Among his key works in Helsinki

INTERNATIONALE
BAUAKADEMIE
BERLIN
EINE FRAGE DER
ARCHITEKTUR

Fig. 11

made in walls—as was previously the case with the immediately adjacent Humboldt Forum, which is to be opened in autumn 2020 in the reconstructed Berliner Stadtschloss or Berlin City Castle—long before the concepts and debates surrounding the actual contents of the Bauakademie are finally agreed.

1 Cf. Zetterberg 2000.
2 Cf. Meyer 2018, p. 30, pp. 42–44.
3 Cf. Meyer 2018, p. 30, pp. 42–44.
4 Cf. Salokorpi 1970, p. 43, pp. 39–40.
5 Arja-Liisa Kaasinen in conversation with the author, May 9, 2019.
6 Riikka Mäkikoskela in conversation with the author, May 13, 2019.
7 Cf. Rambow 2000, p. 62.
8 Cf. Rauterberg 2000 and cf. Klotz 1984.
9 Cf. https://web.archive.org/web/20140201160859/http://www.nba.fi/en/cultural_environment/built_heritage/built_welfare_project/heritage_of_tomorrow (accessed January 11, 2020).
10 Cf. Leitzken 2017a, 2017b, 2018, cf. Fröbe 2014, 2018, cf. Fröbe and Winderlich 2017.
11 Cf. Bundesstiftung Baukultur 2018, p. 1.
12 Among the most successful projects in this respect are the "Stadtentdecker" projects of the Brandenburg Chamber of Architects, which were implemented in 2013.
13 Cf. https://www.iltalehti.fi/helsinki/a/200802267303055 (What's the ugliest building in Helsinki? February 26, 2008), and cf. https://www.iltalehti.fi/helsinki/a/200803117368145 and cf. https://www.uusisuomi.fi/uutiset/suomen-rumin-talo-myytiin/f34dc29f-3b76-38a5-8659-e56de9af9b3c ("Finland's ugliest building is sold" June 9, 2008).
14 Cf. https://fi.wikipedia.org/wiki/Stora_Enson_p%C3%A4%C3%A4konttori (accessed January 16, 2020).
15 Cf. Griffith 1997
16 Cf. Fröbe 2018, pp. 158–169.
17 Cf. *Oodi* information brochure (unpag.).
18 Cf. https://www.csmonitor.com/World/Europe/2019/0124/Welcome-to-Oodi-Helsinki-s-new-living-room (accessed September 15, 2019).
19 Cf. Detlefs 2019.
20 Cf. Detlefs 2019.
21 *Oodi* information brochure (unpag.).
22 Cf. https://www.helmet.fi/enUS/Libraries_and_services/Helsinki_Central_Library_Oodi/Oodis_Facilities/Principles_for_safer_space(177204) (accessed September 15, 2019).
23 Cf. https://www.koeln.de/koeln/makerspace_in_der_zentralbibliothek_eroeffnet_726305.html (accessed January 19, 2020).
24 Cf. Interview with Juha Kaakinen, head of the Finnish NGO Y-Foundation, in *Die Zeit*, March 1, 2018, https://www.zeit.de/gesellschaft/zeitgeschehen/2018-03/ finnland-soziale-gerechtigkeit-grundwohnen-juha-kaakinen-interview (accessed January 16, 2020).
25 Cf. https://minedu.fi/en/article/-/asset_publisher/helsinkiin-suunnitellaan-maailmanluokan-arkkitehtuuri-ja-designmuseota (accessed January 16, 2020).
26 Cf. https://www.uusimuseo.fi/en/ (accessed January 17, 2020).
27 Cf. http://www.bbr.bund.de/SiteGlobals/Functions/Hauptspalte/DE/BBR/Buehne_Box/inhalt/180507_bauakademie_programmwettbewerb.html;jsessionid=21DEA26820B71D7E1047549C6F413A11.live21302 (accessed January 17, 2020) and cf. https://www.tagesspiegel.de/kultur/wiederaufbau-der-schinkelschen-bauakademie-historische-rekonstruktion-oder-blosses-konzept/23952528.html (accessed January 17, 2020).

Finnish architectural policy—a learning process

The Finnish government's architectural policy program, which was officially launched on December 17, 1998, is a small, richly illustrated brochure of only 28 pages, which—and this was both essential and innovative—was the result of an active cooperation between two ministries, the Ministry of Education (which has since then been renamed Ministry of Education and Culture) and the Ministry of the Environment. The process was initiated by the architects' associations and architectural institutions, which had already begun to demand an architectural policy program in the 1980s.[1] The work was carried out under the direction of the National Council for Architecture and the Ministry of Education with the active support of the Finnish Association of Architects SAFA.[2] Two working groups set up by the ministry were responsible for producing the content: from February 1996 to June 1997, the first commission under the direction of Prof. Tore Tallqvist developed the basic outlines of the

Architectural Policy, which were then presented to a wider circle of experts in order to be reviewed and discussed. The results were integrated by a second working group chaired by Pekka Laatio between January and June 1998. On December 17, 1998, the *Architectural Policy* was adopted by the government.[3] The illustrated version, financed by the Ministry of Education and the Arts Council of Finland and designed and edited by SAFA, was first published in Finnish and Swedish in 1999, but was also translated into English, French, and German for release that same year.

In terms of content, it is essentially a self-declaration or an encouragement addressed to the public authorities to set an example and ensure high architectural quality in the construction of public buildings. It was guided by the hope that this would subsequently become reflected in the rest of society.[4] At the same time, the program aims in particular at "creating the necessary conditions for the realization of the fundamental rights to a healthy environment that are enshrined in the Finnish Constitution. This not only requires knowledge about architecture and the built environment, but also of ways to influence both," as stated in the foreword to the *Architectural Policy* by Paavo Lipponen, then prime minister of Finland.[5]

The remarkably generalized text begins by formulating the objectives of the *Architectural Policy* and describes the social, cultural, but also economic values of architecture. Lipponen states that architecture creates the broad framework for people's lives but is also capable of creating national and local identity and can refine given natural conditions into a cultural landscape. Due to its long lifespan, it thus also creates lasting values for the nation's wealth, which will gradually turn into the cultural heritage of tomorrow.[6]

In total, the program consists of seven short chapters, which lay out the 24 commented decisions. A particularly prominent part is devoted to the topic "culture and education," which is also reflected in the fact that ten of the 24 decisions can be found in this chapter. The first four decisions (7-10) relate to the handling of the architectural heritage and the protection of historical monuments. Before dealing with the topic of "basic education," a subchapter explains that the intention is to strengthen the role of architecture as a component of art and culture, since architecture is a central and sensually perceptible form of culture. "Our national identity," it continues, "has often found its permanent expression in architecture. Through buildings we have shown the vitality and uniqueness of our culture. ... Moreover, the most internationally known examples of our culture are often buildings."[7] The following paragraph on "general education" states that the understanding of architecture should be part of the general education of every mature citizen. It criticizes architecture education in schools as inadequate, not least due to a lack of teaching materials. However, an existing law on Basic Education in the Arts provides a good basis for establishing architecture at various levels of education. Furthermore, it is agreed that building culture should play a more central role in teacher training: "The key to understanding architecture," it goes on to say, "lies primarily in art education as well as in environment-related subjects that incorporate the concerns of the built environment. The citizens' ability to participate in the decision-making processes that affect their immediate environment can be greatly enhanced when architecture becomes a part of the curriculum of environmental studies, biology, geography, history, or political science.[8] In the following resolutions it is stated:

"(Decision 12)
In establishing the curricula, the Central Office of Education will emphasize the importance of architectural education. In addition, the need for an understanding of architecture will be taken into account when interweaving school education and cultural life."

"(Decision 13)
The Ministry of Education will examine the possibilities of developing architectural education within the framework of adult education in order to improve the citizens' ability to influence decision-making processes concerning their immediate environment."

"(Decision 14)
Decision-makers, elected representatives, and representatives of local authorities shall be offered training in the fields of architecture and the environment."[9]

In addition, it was decided to improve training in the construction sector and to incorporate the fundamentals of architectural and building history into vocational training at all levels (decision 15). Furthermore, the training of architects should include the possibility to supplement research activities with experimental planning and building exercises (decision 16), and the chance to conduct architectural research should be improved (decision 17).[10]

The particular economic importance of construction and its drastic and lasting effects on the environment require that consumer protection is improved, as stated in the chapter on architecture and quality of construction. To this end, "an increase in quality, paired with the principles of sustainable development, is sought out, with a particular emphasis on issues of health, functionality, aesthetics, and a clear responsibility."[11] This is for instance to be achieved by holding more competitions, as these on the one hand promote innovation and are on the other also a form of further training and thus open up opportunities for young architects. "The wide range of alternative solutions offered by a competition facilitates a public debate."[12] In order to increase the public awareness of architecture, the program plans to award grants and prizes, but also seeks to strengthen the role of the Museum of Finnish Architecture and encourage the participation in international exhibitions, publications, or events.[13] In the last part, which deals with the implementation of the *Architectural Policy,* it becomes clear that for the involved actors, the thus formulated *Architectural Policy* is by no means the final step but is on the contrary seen as the beginning of the actual work.[14]

The specifics of Finland's Architectural Policy from 1998

What clearly contributed to the success of the Finnish *Architectural Policy* was the fact that it was flanked by concrete measures that ensured that it did not merely remain a document or a declaration of intent. For example, the work on the national architectural policy program was given an additional boost by the simultaneous renewal process of the Land Use and Building Act. This new act came into force in the beginning of 2000 and created the legal basis both for a better participation in planning processes and for the preservation of built cultural heritage.[15] In June 2001, this was followed by the *National Strategy for Built Heritage*, which Paavo Lipponen considered to be one of the most significant consequences of the 1998 *Architectural Policy*.[16] It is interesting to note that supporting measures have not only accompanied the *Architectural Policy*, but that the program itself was conceived and communicated as an accompanying measure. As early as 1995, in the course of the reform of fundamental rights legislation, the right to a healthy living environment, to which civic duties are also linked, was integrated into the Finnish catalog of fundamental rights and anchored in the new Finnish constitution in 1999.[17] This embedding and interlocking of the *Architectural Policy* with other programs and legislative procedures at various levels has certainly made a major contribution to the fact that the Finnish *Architectural Policy* has not stood the test of time on paper alone, but that many aspects have been successfully implemented, as will be shown later.

It is also remarkable that a balancing act between maximum openness on the one hand and precise concretization on the other has been achieved within the architectural policy program. The text is formulated in such a general and fundamental way that it is likely to be met with broad approval. As Tiina Valpola, founding director of the Architecture Information Centre Finland (Archinfo Finland), set out in an interview, it also contains the reasons why the 1998 architectural policy program received such wide international attention: "Essentially, anyone could sign this text. It still holds up, even if, from today's point of view, some things are of course missing."[18] What this means is that this brief text describes the social, cultural, and economic values of architecture and convincingly outlines the importance of the built environment for each individual but also for society as the overarching cultural achievement. The fact that these statements are not only valid in Finland, but apply everywhere, is also reflected in the fact that the *Architectural Policy* was, quite surprisingly, translated into Arabic in 2007.[19] (Fig. 12) At the same time, the document is concise in that it essentially instigates the public authorities' voluntary commitment to act in an exemplary manner when tasked with designing buildings as well as to initiate competitions whenever possible and to enable the highest levels of innovation and quality. This approach is rather obvious since the options to intervene in a controlling manner are in fact given in this context.

The rather open and general text is complemented by 24 decisions, two thirds of which are so specific that they even name an addressee who is responsible for checking or implementing them. At times, the text merely makes use of terms such as "contracting authorities" or "public offices." In most cases, however, the responsible entity is directly named—be it the Ministry of Education, the National Board of Education, the Ministry of the Environment, the National Board of Antiquities, the Museum of Finnish Architecture, or the Academy of Finland. Quite possibly this concretization has led to the successful implementation of large parts of the *Architectural Policy*. This assumption has been questioned by Tiina Valpola, who in conversation expressed an opposing view. She complained that the *Architectural Policy* of 1998 was not drawn up clearly enough. In her opinion, the state used the document primarily to encourage itself to act as a role model. The problem was, according to Valpola, that the tasks and responsibilities for implementing and executing the measures were not defined clearly enough. As a result, it remained impossible to reach all relevant actors in the construction industry.[20] During the conversation, Petra Havu shared Valpola's view and also described the

1 هدف السياسة المعمارية

تهدف الحكومة من برنامج "السياسة المعمارية" إلى تحديد الأطر والأهداف المعمارية لتنفيذها بواسطة الأجهزة الرسمية. فتضع تلك السياسة المعمارية الإرشادات لحماية تراثنا المعماري، وصيانة ثروتنا المعمارية والإرتقاء بها، وتوفر فرصاً لتعزيز معايير معمارية عالية المستوى للبناء، وتحسّن قدرة قطاع الإنشاءات لدينا على المنافسة الفعالة في محيط عالمي أوسع.

وللعمارة قيم اجتماعية وثقافية واقتصادية عظيمة، وهي جزء مهم من ثقافتنا القومية. .ونستطيع بواسطة العمارة إن نوفر للمواطنين بيئة جيدة قابلة للعيش فيها – فمن حق كل مواطن أن يتمتع ببيئة معيشية جيدة – وعمارة راقية. ومن واجب كل مؤسسة عامة أن تعمل لإحقاق هذه الحقوق..

وكما تهدف السياسة المعمارية للإرتقاء بمستوى الإنشاء،فإنها تؤصل لمبادئ التنمية المستدامة فيما يخص استخدام الأراضي وإنشاءات المباني. هذا بالإضافة إلى أنها تتبنى الشفافية، والتفاعل بين الأطراف المعنية، وهي نفس أهداف الإصلاحات الجديدة لقوانين استخدام الأراضي والبناء.

1.1 ما هي العمارة؟

يرتكز التعريف التقليدي للعمارة على ثلاثة أركان: الإستفادة، الديمومة، الجمال. وما تزال هذه الأركان الثلاثة صالحة الآن، بالرغم من أن الزمن الحاضر قد أضاف إليها منظورا جديداً.

فتشمل الإستفادة، الأداء والفائدة العملية والاستخدام الإقتصادي للمصادر. أما مفهوم الديمومة فقد توسع من مجرد متانة الإنشاء ليشمل الديمومة البيئية. إلا أنه لابد من التركيزعلى الإستزادة من قيم الجمال والراحة في البيئات العمرانية بشكل أكبر مما هو حاصل في الحاضر.

وترتبط العمارة بالزمان والمكان. فيربط الزمان المباني ببيئاتها المحيطة ويخلق تراثاً ثقافياً وتاريخاً. أما المكان فيعطي معنى للعلاقة بين العمارة ومحيطها المباشر والبيئة الطبيعية بشكل عام.

1. محطة مراقبة الطيور في مركز خليج ليمينكا (Liminganlahti).
تكوّن الظروف الطبيعية والعمارة مجتمعتين المنظر الثقافي الطبيعي الذي يعبر عن التراث وقيم المجتمع. ويشكّل البحر مصدراً للغذاء لكل من الإنسان والطير. وملاذ الطيور في مياه خليج ليمينكا جزء من برنامج الإتحاد الأوروبي لحماية الطبيعة. وقد تم تنفيذ المبنى الذي يتميز باحترام للطبيعة، بتمويل جزئي من الإتحاد الأوروبي.
(Maija Niemelä) مايّا نيميلا و (Pentti Myllymäki) بينتي مولوماكي، 1998.

Fig. 12

2

يتحقق الإبداع المعماري من خلال المقياس، والأشكال، وعلاقة الفضاءات، والهيكلية، واختيار المواد، وتصميم التفاصيل، والتنفيذ الدقيق، بالإضافة لعوامل أخرى. وتتأتى أهمية العمارة من أن البيئة العمرانية تشكل الإطار العضوي للنشاط الإنساني، مما يجعل دور العمارة أساسياً في تحديد قيمة البيئة.

كما ترتبط بالعمارة أيضاً قيم ومعان قوية وهذه تشكل الهوية الوطنية والمحلية. حيث أن تأثير العمارة يمتد لمدى طويل، لذا فإنها توجد قيماً ثابتة.

تشكل البيئات الثقافية للمدن والريف ثروتنا، وهناك مراحل تاريخية متعددة لمدننا يجب الحفاظ عليها. ويشكّل المنظر الثقافي الطبيعي الذي يتألف من المباني والبيئة الطبيعية جزءاً أساساً من قيمة الريف.

1.2 البيئة الجيدة حق أساس لكل مواطن

وقد أدى التنامي في الوعي البيئي والاهتمام بالبيئة الطبيعية إلى تغير العلاقة بين الناس والمحيط الذي يعيشون فيه، وزادت الحاجة لتطوير أساليب حياة وبيئات معيشة تتماشى مع مفهوم التنمية المستديمة..

ويضمن برنامج حكومتنا الحق الأساس لكل مواطن في بيئة صحية، وإتاحة الفرصة للمواطن للتأثير على صنع القرار فيما يخص البيئة. ومن جهة أخرى فإنه يفرض على المواطن تحمل مسئوليته عن البيئة والتراث الثقافي. وتعضد السياسات المعمارية للحكومة تحقيق هذه الحقوق.

MV/Maija Niemelä

3

تعتبر الفرصة الحقيقية للحوار بين صانع القرار والشعب عنصراً رئيساً في تحقيق المجتمع المدني الذي يكون المواطن في مركزه. ولتحقيق هذا الهدف لابد من وجود أنظمة صنع قرار منفتحة ومواطنين يمتلكون الوعي والرغبة في المشاركة. ولقد ازدادت أهمية المشاركة الشعبية خصوصاً في الأمور التي تتعلق بالبيئة بصورة كبيرة. وتتكامل مشاركة المواطنين ونشاطاتهم المستقلة مع الثقافة التقليدية للحكومة فيما يخص خطط استخدامات الأراضي والبناء.

وبالإضافة لذلك، تتطلب المسئولية تجاه التراث الثقافي أن يزداد اهتمام صانع القرار المسئول عن أمور التخطيط والبناء على مستوى البلديات بالحفاظ على القيم الثقافية والجمالية للمباني القائمة وبيئاتها المباشرة.

implementation as a weakness of the first policy: "We set up a nice program, but the implementation did not go as well as one would have wished."[21]

According to Tiina Valpola, the implementation process until 2011 took place in two waves. In the first phase, which according to her ran from 1998 to 2003, implementation progressed rapidly and, after a brief period of stagnation, gained momentum again from 2004 onwards.[22] During the first phase, the process was actively accompanied by the Finnish Association of Architects SAFA in close cooperation with the National Council for Architecture with the aim of raising awareness of the *Architectural Policy* throughout the country. These public relations measures, coordinated by Heini Korpelainen, resulted in an illustrated publication of the program and about 50 events providing information were organized throughout the country.[23] Korpelainen was also managing director of the monitoring group that produced the 2002 *Follow-up Report* ("Valtioneuvoston arkkitehtuu-ripoliittisen ohjelman toteutumisen seuranta ja jatkotoimenpiteet") on the implementation of the *Architectural Policy*.[24] This report was commissioned by the Ministry of Education and Culture in June 1999 and presented three years later, in June 2002. The report of a working group consisting of 13 members confirms that the implementation in the first three years was quite successful, although only nine of the total of 24 measures had been implemented at the time. In the case of the measures that had not yet been implemented, the contact partners had either not been identified correctly or had not yet been identified at all, as can be read in the report's summary.[25]

The monitoring group considered it a success that the program put architecture on the political agenda and that a process involving many responsible actors was initiated throughout the country. The monitoring and evaluation phase also brought a wide variety of actors together and thus initiated a valuable learning process.[26] Overall, the implementation of the *Architectural Policy* measures in the area of "culture and education" was assessed positively, although it entailed certain limitations. Measure 11, for instance, was designed to improve the position of architecture within the arts and culture of Finland and was assessed as generally successful—it included the founding of the Alvar Aalto Academy—and yet the authors point out that the Ministry of Education and Culture has in recent years suffered budget cuts.[27] In a similar way, measure 12, by means of which architecture education should be integrated into school curricula, has also made progress and will be further developed. It is, however, explicitly pointed out that not enough advanced training opportunities are available for teachers.[28] The report also indicates that measures 13 to 15 have not progressed according to the working group's assessment: it has not yet been possible to integrate architecture education into adult education, to provide further training for decision-makers and elected representatives of local authorities, and to strengthen the foundations of architectural and building history in vocational training. Measure 16, which is dedicated to the training of architects, also requires further actions to be taken to create actual possibilities for supplementing research activities with experimental planning and building exercises.[29]

Since only nine of the 24 measures have so far been successfully implemented, the monitoring group recommends continuing the work on architectural policy and has proposed nine follow-up measures. These include, among other things, the idea of publishing a new report every three years, which will document the progress made in implementing the architectural policy program.[30] Furthermore, the authors advocate the establishment of an "Information and Promotion Centre" for architecture, whose core tasks would include the promotion of Finnish architecture and culture but also an improvement in the country's architectural awareness (demand 6). Under 7 and 8, the demands of the 1998 architectural policy program are explicitly renewed, which envision an intensified architecture education in school curricula, in the adult education sector as well as in the training of politicians and decision-makers.[31]

A second report, *Discovering Architecture. Civic Education in Architecture in Finland,* published by the Finnish Association of Architects SAFA and the Arts Council of Finland (now the Arts Promotion Centre) in 2001, shows how well advanced the field of architecture education already was in Finland at this point. It will be examined in more detail in a later chapter of this study. In the course of this first phase, numerous architecture education projects made possible by the funding policy of the Ministry of Education and the National Council for Architecture were carried out,[32] so that even at this early stage the authors of the study were aware of about 200 projects throughout Finland.[33]

Local and regional architectural policies

One of the most important successes of the Finnish *Architectural Policy* of 1998 was an aspect that only became a major issue during the second wave of implementation: as a result of the national *Architectural Policy,* local architectural policies have been developed on a voluntary basis in twelve cities and five regions of Finland, some of which have already gone through a round of revisions. This is surprising in that there were no indications or recommendations whatsoever in the national *Architectural Policy,* as Tiina Valpola pointed out in a lecture held in Luxembourg in November 2015.[34] The first local programs already emerged during the first implementation wave: as early as 2000, the province of Eastern Finland had created a tailor-made regional program, and in 2002 the cities of Jyväskylä and Oulu were the first to adopt their own local architectural policies. The fact that ten more cities and four regions followed suit in the second wave of implementation was a result of an active information policy instigated by the Ministry of Education. After a period of stagnation in 2003 resulting from the publication of the *Follow-up Report,* the ministry became active in 2004 and delegated the responsibility for the further implementation and promotion of the *Architectural Policy* to the National Council for Architecture (now the National Council for Architecture and Design) which, under the chairmanship of Anna Brunow, set up a special advisor for architecture with the aim, among other things, of promoting national architectural policies at the local and regional level.[35] This post was held by Tiina Valpola from 2004 to 2012, when the Architecture Information Centre Finland (Archinfo Finland) was established. Valpola was at the time already involved in the implementation process of the national *Architectural Policy* as an active member of the Finnish Association of Architects SAFA and was also a board member of three of the five founding institutions, SAFA, the Museum of Finnish Architecture, and the Building Information Foundation.[36] Under Valpola's direction, from 2004 to 2011, the implementation process gained a new dynamic: "The activities changed; they became more visible and their range broadened radically. We no longer focused on the presentation of the policy document, but instead started to promote activities at the grassroots level in

Municipal Programmes

- completed / accepted by the city council or board
- in preparation
- pending

Regional Programmes

- completed
- in preparation
- pending

ARCHITECTURE POLICY SEMINARS

Discussing Architectural Quality
Helsinki 21.5.2002

1. Moniääninen suunnittelu – Arkkitehtuuripoliittiset ohjelmat kuntien ja julkishallinnon työvälineenä
Helsinki 3.12.2004

2. Tulevaisuuskuvia, arjen työvälineitä vai sitovia toimintaohjeita – kohtauspaikka arkkitehtuuripoliittisia ohjelmia laativille kunnille ja alueille **Helsinki 12.1.2006**

Celebrating the Everyday – Aspects of Architectural Policies
Helsinki 19–21.10.2006

3. Kokonaisvaltaista ja kestävää! Paikkojen ja seutujen uudet haasteet
Helsinki 24.9.2008

4. Arkipäivän arkkitehtuuripolitiikka: Nostetta paikkojen ja seutujen kehittämiseen **Oulu 27.11.2009**

5. Rakennetun ympäristön kulttuuri kehitysvoimana **Savonlinna 21.9.2010**

6. Does the built environment need new kind of quality catalysts?
Helsinki 23.9.2010

7. Cities for People – yleisöluennot
Turku 17.3.2011

8. Kaupunki rakentuu rannoiltaan – Kohtaavatko odotukset? **Turku 29.9.2011**

Järjestäjänä valtion rakennustaidetoimikunta yhteistyössä OKM:n ja YM:n kanssa.

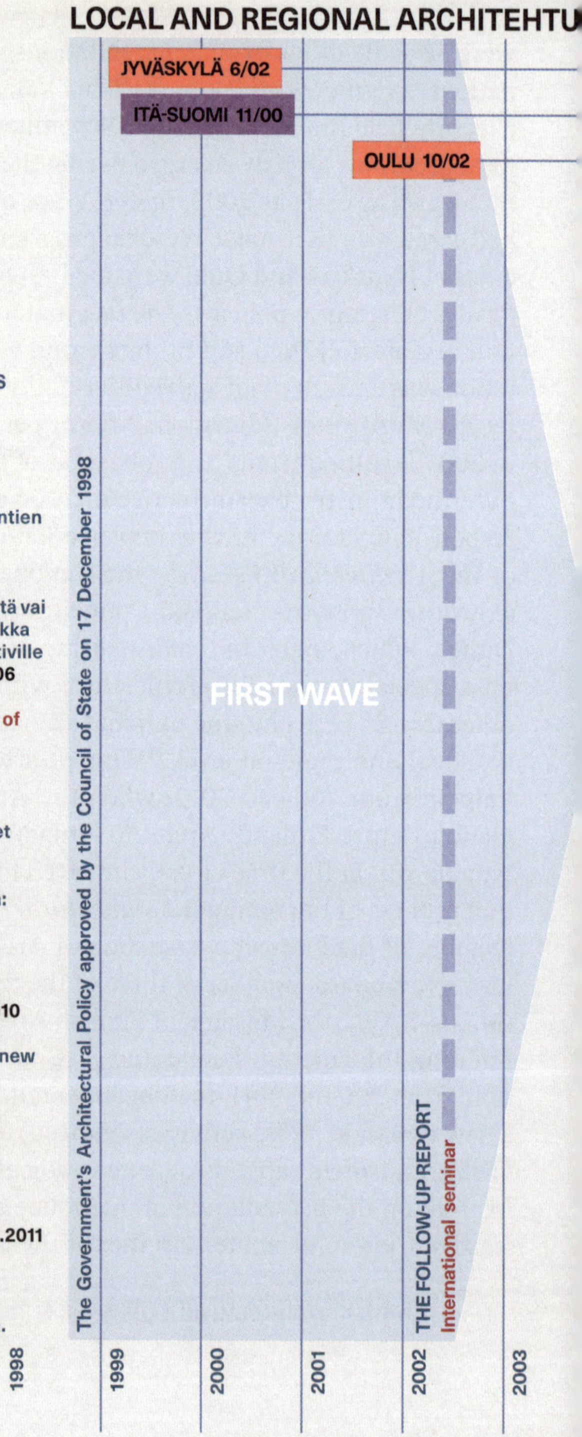

Fig. 13

POLICY PROGRAMMES IN FINLAND

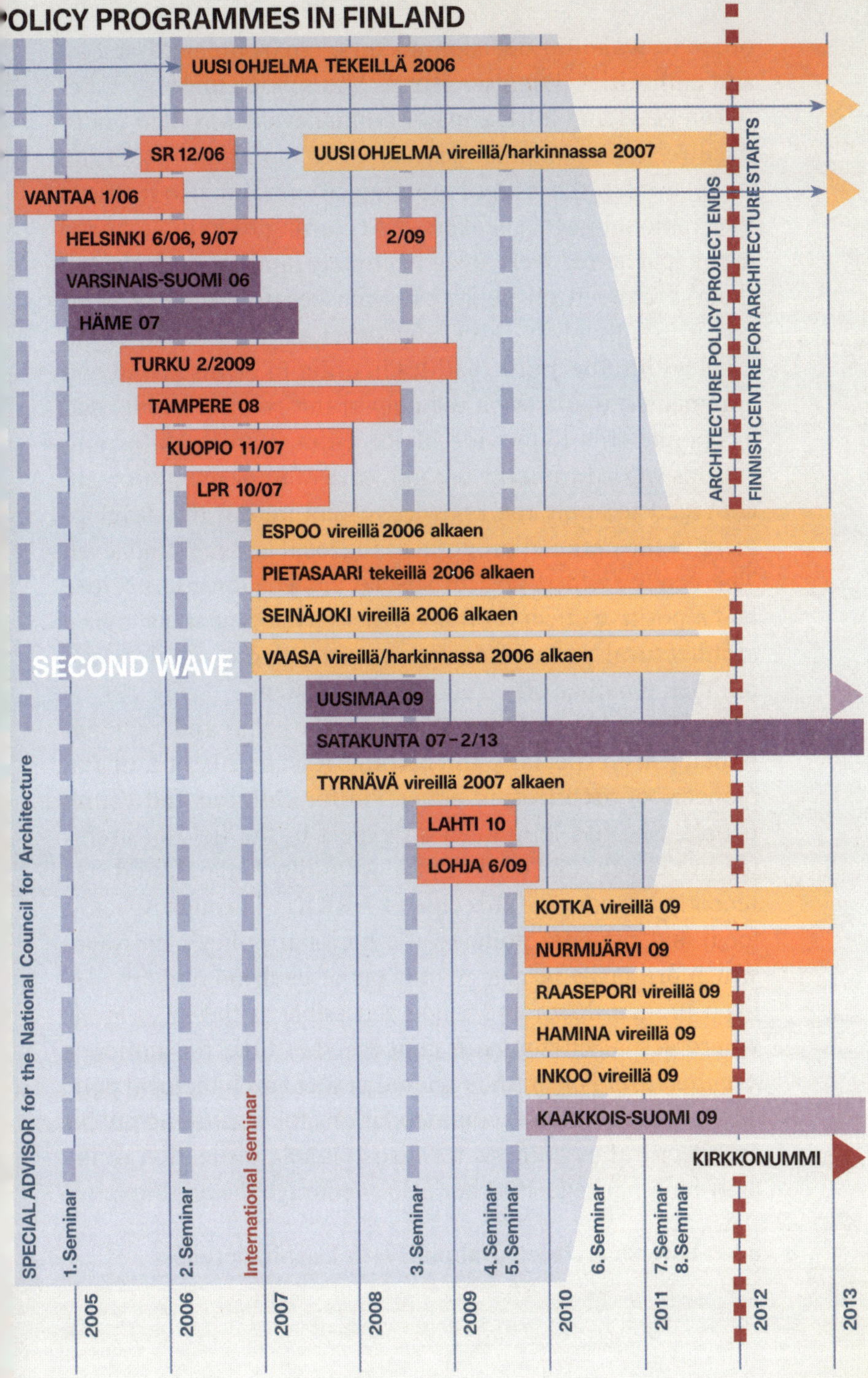

order to wake up decision-makers, environmental actors, and authorities, but also citizens and schoolchildren."[37] Between 2004 and 2011, a major annual event was held under the direction of Valpola: this addressed municipal actors and key players in the field of building culture but also featured international guest speakers.[38] According to Valpola, many municipal actors were by now already familiar with the national architectural policy program because draft versions had, throughout its three-year development period, circulated within the municipalities in order to be discussed and commented upon. With the help of informative events and a concrete offer to provide advice, cities, municipalities, and regions were during the second wave of implementation encouraged to apply the knowledge acquired in the development of the national program at the local and regional level. The newly created post of special advisor for architecture had a positive effect on this further development, as it gave architectural policy a direct contact person—a telephone number, email or office address, for instance.[39] (Fig. 13)

According to Jaana Räsänen, the local and regional policies are especially interesting. Räsänen is one of the pioneers of architecture education for children and young people. She has long been an expert in the field of architecture education, working for Archinfo Finland, and has recently become the director of ARKKI. Through specific local and regional policies, the national policy's message, which primarily targets politicians or decision-makers, has been broken down and made accessible at the local level, where actual citizens are concerned.[40] Like the national *Architectural Policy*, the regional or local architectural policies usually contain recommendations for improving public architectural awareness, for a sustainable protection of locally built heritage, but they also encourage the organization of competitions and the architecture education of children and young people. What they also have in common is that they have the potential to improve the regional and local self-esteem of both citizens and politicians.[41] According to Valpola, however, the effectiveness of local architectural policies varies from city to city. Some municipalities have, for instance, successfully integrated local architectural policies into other development strategies and have thus used them as "collaborative learning platforms." In some cases—and this must be said in all honesty—these policies have tended to remain a cultural proclamation or statement of intent rather than a practical catalyst. One can, generally, conclude that the process was always more important than the document itself, since during the approximately two years of developing the publication, there was an unprecedented amount of discourse and debate on architecture and building culture.[42] Petri Tuormala also comes to this conclusion in his study on local and regional architectural policy programs in Finland.[43]

According to Valpola, the idea that local and regional architectural policy processes have been quite useful for municipalities also manifests itself in the fact that cities such as Vantaa (2015), Kuopio (2017), Oulu (2017), or Jyväskylä (2019) have already launched a second generation of local architectural policies while the city of Helsinki is actively working on a new edition, and Tampere is discussing one.[44] What the second generation of architectural policies have in common is that they are even more individually tailored to each of these cities and are therefore more concrete and more interactive than previous programs. Valpola explains the continuing interest in architectural policy programs by pointing out that the new demands for interaction and participation require both new actors and a shared knowledge base.

But the competition among various municipalities could also be an underlying reason and, in addition, urban development has in the last two decades become increasingly complicated so that a strategic framework for setting clear goals is definitely needed. What is further noticeable is that the construction industry is increasingly interested in forms of political cooperation, as a growing number of clients appears to be more quality-conscious than ever.[45]

With the establishment of Archinfo Finland in 2013, to be discussed in greater detail in the following chapter, consultancy work in the regions and municipalities continued, and the idea of revising national architectural policy also gained new impetus. In her position as special advisor for architecture for the National Council for Architecture, Tiina Valpola had already initiated a renewal process. In an unpublished paper, which Valpola presented at the EFAP conference in Gdańsk in November 2011, she argued that, shortly after the publication of the 1998 national *Architectural Policy*, the call for reform was heard and heeded for almost the entire decade.[46] The impetus for this was certainly provided by the 2002 *Follow-up Report* which clearly showed that changes could be identified in only nine of the 24 areas.[47] The 2008 Annual Report to the Ministry of Education and Culture, from which Tiina Valpola has kindly provided translated extracts, shows how far the process had already progressed in the course of that year. According to the report, the informal Apoli2 working group, which was made up of twelve representatives from the Ministry of Education, the Ministry for the Environment, the National Council for Architecture, and the Finnish Association of Architects SAFA, met several times in 2008 and in the following year welcomed the Regional Development Department of the Ministry of Economic Affairs and Employment as a new cooperation partner. In 2010 and 2011, three workshops organized by the Ministry of the Environment were held, the last of which was part of an international conference.[48]

Despite the good visibility that the Apoli2 work achieved at the administrative level and despite the working group's active groundwork, Valpola stated that they did not succeed in supplying the architectural policy reform with an official status, partly due to the extensive organizational reforms in the ministries and the resulting changes in job descriptions.[49] In an email from December 21, 2019, Valpola writes about the "Apoli2 process that came to nothing," adding that "in retrospect, the process was hampered by structural changes in the ministries' organization and their senior officials, particularly the Ministry of the Environment. The fluctuation of the ministries' representatives involved in the working group and the lack of clear responsibilities also proved to be difficult. Nevertheless, the ministries continued to work together, for example in the context of promoting local architectural policies or by participating in events hosted by the European Forum for Architectural Policies network."[50] According to Valpola, the Ministry of Education and Culture was clearly committed to continuing a process of revising the architectural policy: "It was also a process that took a few years because the ministry first had to allocate financial resources for its work."[51] As a consequence, the work on a new architectural policy could not begin until 2016, when it was again taken up under the direction of Archinfo Finland's new executive director, Hanna Harris. A revision of the architectural policy has become necessary, states the Ministry of Education and Culture's website with regard to the newly launched APOLI2020 process, because: "While the program has made progress at the local level in recent years, the national program has never been updated."[52]

APOLI2020

In May 2019, the plan to revise the national architectural policy was announced. A new architectural policy program, named APOLI2020, is intended to be developed by fall 2020. When asked why a new program was needed, Petra Havu, a counsellor for cultural affairs in the Ministry of Education and Culture's Department of Arts and Cultural Policy and therefore in charge of organizing the APOLI2020 development, replied: "Here in Finland, we face the challenge that our architectural policy was developed 20 years ago and is dated. We no longer have a network. ... 20 years is simply a long time. Society has changed—not completely, but it definitely has changed—and because the document is so old it loses its validity because the conditions around it have changed so much. A 20-year-old architectural policy is too old to be implemented—because not everything has been implemented yet! ... We also have a new government, new ministers—and, of course, they want to make their own political changes. In addition, today other issues than 20 years ago are important—issues that are not tied to governments."[53] Havu reported that a completely new network had to be built in order to establish the APOLI2020 process because the actors who developed the *Architectural Policy* 20 years ago are today either retired or work elsewhere. "Without a network and mostly people who are not used to work together, it is very difficult to find the right partners to build up a strong cooperation. In Finland, each ministry works independently—yet we have now been able to build a strong relationship with the Ministry of Environment and have found the right partners with whom we cooperate very well. At the beginning, however, this process proved very laborious. We had to negotiate a lot of things and meet with employees from all different levels. You have to create a shared understanding. This is a time-consuming effort, especially because we are all rather busy and could only move forward taking very small steps."[54]

The website of the Ministry of Education and Culture provides information on the new working group and its 21 permanent members who offer a wide range of expertise on the built environment.[55] There are, in addition, plans to consult further experts and involve stakeholders in the process. The development process will predominantly be overseen by Archinfo Finland, with Riitta Kaivosoja, general manager of the Ministry of Education and Culture, as its first chairperson, and Senior Ministerial Adviser Petra Havu from the Ministry of Education and Culture and Senior Architect Harri Hakaste from the Ministry of the Environment as vice chairs.[56]

Hanna Harris, director of Archinfo Finland, which has been in charge of the whole process since 2016, reported in a personal conversation on the lengthy preparatory work that had taken place in the run-up to the actual policy work. The conference "More Architecture—Architecture as a Resource for Nordic Culture," which took place in Helsinki in October 2016, marked the beginning of the conversation between the Ministry of Education and Culture and Archinfo Finland. After this conference, Archinfo Finland was commissioned by the ministry to conduct a preliminary study: it was agreed that 25 key persons should be interviewed in order to find out whether an architectural policy is still relevant today and, if so, which issues are currently of particular importance. Harris explains that after the preliminary study was published in 2017,[57] a first round of discussions within the ministry was organized before they were gradually extended to the Ministry of the Environment. She states that this process taught her that it is indeed possible to bring different positions together, but that it takes time and needs the right focus. Harris elaborates that a variety of round table discussions with a group of ten to twelve people were organized in the course of a year. It was not until the end of April 2019 that a collective decision was made to initiate a new development process.

The website of the Ministry of Education and Culture lists the following keywords as topics to be considered in the APOLI2020 process:

+ "Sustainable development and life-cycle approach
+ Health and wellbeing
+ Equality, non-discrimination and inclusivity
+ Digitalisation, new technologies and innovative thinking
+ Demographic change, regional development and migration
+ Prominence, competitiveness, and export of Finnish architecture
+ Cultural heritage and cultural tourism
+ Critique, theory and research of architecture
+ Architectural education and training."[58]

Harris explains that it is APOLI2020's declared goal to provide more extensive support for the development of local architectural policies and to involve more local actors—including schools, since school policy is determined at local level.[59] The fact that architecture education will also play an important role in the new national architectural policy has already been indicated in the preliminary study *Tulevaisuuden suomea Rakentamassa. Arkkitehtuuripolitiikan uudistamisen suuntaviivoja* (Shaping the Future of Finland.

Guidelines for the Reform of the Architectural Policy), in which the topic plays a central role. The study stresses the importance of giving children and adolescents in kindergartens, elementary and secondary schools access to the world of architecture.[60] Yet there are new challenges, for instance that the integration of architecture into the new curriculum for community schools, which came into force in 2016, has apparently become more difficult, since the architecture course, which was designed to be taught in art classes from grade 1-7 level, was cut. At the same time, the new curriculum emphasizes interdisciplinary, phenomena-oriented learning, which suits architecture as an essentially interdisciplinary topic.[61] Representatives from the municipal level also identified the need for further development in order to facilitate access to architecture education. Although much progress has recently been made at this level, it is mainly achieved in university towns where architects or teachers are trained. Architecture as part of the Basic Education in the Arts is only offered in the metropolitan region, in Jyväskylä or the Gulf of Lapland. Everywhere else, only short-term projects are available.[62] In light of the current Land Use and Building Act, which grants citizens the right to co-determination, there is a renewed call to integrate architecture education into adult education, but also to train politicians and decision-makers—as had already been called for in 1998.[63] According to Mikko Hartikainen, who represents the Finnish National Agency of Education in the APOLI2020 working group, it is to be expected that the participation of children and young people in real planning processes will be intensified.[64] One major innovation, states Harris, is that the construction industry will for the first time be involved in such a process, which is essential for the debate around equality and sustainability.[65] A total of four workshops are planned; the final one in spring 2020 is devoted to the topic of architecture education, as Eeva Astala of Archinfo Finland reported.[66] According to Petra Havu, one of the most important goals of the new architectural policy is a greater focus on implementation, whose lack can be viewed as the first policy's weakness. This is why it is so important that all relevant actors and organizations are from the very beginning involved in the process and can thus build a sustainable network: "In the end, it is not about writing a text but about the process and the people. A network must be built and maintained. The real work starts only after the document has been adopted."[67]

Conclusion: Processes in architectural policy

If the German *Guidelines for Baukultur* are to become not only a "cultural proclamation" but a "catalyst," in Tiina Valpola's words, Germany can learn a lot from the Finnish experience of developing, implementing, and revising architectural policy processes. The APOLI2020 process currently underway and its failed predecessor Apoli2 offer a glimpse into the difficult and lengthy processes that precede such a development. It also shows the enormous efforts that are required in advance, even before the actual design process takes shape. This example shows that the initial conditions for inter-ministerial cooperation in Finland were probably by no means more favorable than in Germany or anywhere else in the world.

The implementation process of the 1998 *Architectural Policy* illustrates, on the one hand, that clear areas of responsibility must be defined and shows, on the other hand, that the implementation process does not happen naturally but must be carefully orchestrated in order to be successful. It requires actors such as the Finnish special advisor for architecture for the National Council for Architecture who communicates the architectural policy measures and acts as a contact person and advisor when it comes to adjusting the architectural policy measures for the federal states, regions, and municipalities. What also proves helpful is, where possible, a central institution comparable to Archinfo Finland that can take responsibility for the processes and pool knowledge. The conditions for such a development are promising in Germany, as it is already equipped with an extensive network of Baukultur associations, networks, and foundations at the federal, state, and local levels, above all the Federal Foundation of Baukultur, which could certainly become a cooperation partner.

For Germany, one of the most interesting aspects of the Finnish architectural policy is the issue of local and regional architectural policies, which volunteers have started up as a result of the national program. This is significant with regard to Germany because here the federal system essentially calls into question an overarching federal Baukultur strategy. Germany can look at Finland's national *Architectural Policy* of 1998 to learn how to develop a federal strategy that is formulated in such an open and general way that it invites appropriation at the federal state level, but also in regions and municipalities. The German *Guidelines for Baukultur* should therefore be as simple and clear as those formulated in Finland in 1998. They should define principles, formulate an attitude towards building culture and should—very importantly—strengthen the role of architecture as an artistic and cultural achievement. Like the 1998 *Architectural Policy*, the German *Guidelines for Baukultur* should first of all be a self-declaration and should appear inviting to the federal states, regions, and municipalities.

1 Cf. Screenshots provided by Tiina Valpola via the now defunct website www.apoli.fi/etusivu. Tiina Valpola wrote the content while working as a special advisor for the National Council for Architecture between 2004 and 2012. Cf. Valpola 2011, p. 3.

2 Tiina Valpola via email, December 19, 2019.

3 Cf. Architectural Policy 1999, p. 2 (unpag.) Tallqvist and Laatio were directors of the National Council for Architecture while working on the publication.

4 Cf. Architectural Policy 1999, pp. 7–9.

5 Cf. Architectural Policy 1999, p. 3.

6 Cf. Architectural Policy 1999, pp. 5–7.

7 Cf. Architectural Policy 1999, p. 15.

8 Cf. Architectural Policy 1999, p. 16.

9 Cf. Architectural Policy 1999, p. 16.

10 Cf. Architectural Policy 1999, pp. 17–19.

11 Cf. Architectural Policy 1999, p. 19.

12 Cf. Architectural Policy 1999, p. 24.

13 Cf. Architectural Policy 1999, p. 24.

14 Cf. Architectural Policy 1999, p. 28.

15 Cf. Valpola 2011, p. 9 and cf. https://www.ym.fi/en-US/Land_use_and_building/Legislation_and_instructions (accessed January 8, 2020).

16 Cf. Hautajärvim 2005, p. 20.

17 2nd Section 20 – Responsibility for the environment: Nature and its biodiversity, the environment and the national heritage are the responsibility of everyone. The public authorities shall endeavor to guarantee for everyone the right to a healthy environment and for everyone the possibility to influence the decisions that concern their own living environment. Cf. http://www.finlex.fi/fi/laki/kaannokset/1999/en19990731.pdf (accessed January 8, 2020).

18 Tiina Valpola in conversation with the author, May 8, 2019.

19 Cf. Valpola 2011, p. 27. Cf. http://archinfo.fi/wp-content/uploads/2014/02/ARABIC.pdf (accessed January 8, 2020).

20 Tiina Valpola in conversation with the author, May 8, 2019.

21 Petra Havu in conversation with the author, May 6, 2019.

22 Cf. Valpola 2011, p. 16.

23 Tiina Valpola via email, December 20, 2019.

24 Tiina Valpola via email, December 19, 2019; cf. Follow-up report 2002.

25 Cf. Monitoring Group 2002, p. 2.

26 Cf. Monitoring Group 2002, p. 7.

27 Cf. Monitoring Group 2002, p. 14.

28 Cf. Monitoring Group 2002, p. 14.

29 Cf. Monitoring Group 2002, pp. 15–16.

30 Cf. Monitoring Group 2002, p. 25.

31 Cf. Monitoring Group 2002, p. 27.

32 Tiina Valpola via email, December 19, 2019.

33 Cf. Korpelainen and Yanar 2001, p. 6.

34 Cf. Valpola 2015, p. 8.

35 Cf. Valpola 2011, p. 16.

36 Tiina Valpola in phone conversation, January 12, 2020.

37 Tiina Valpola via email, December 20, 2019.

38 Cf. Valpola 2015, pp. 12–13.

39 Cf. Valpola 2015, pp. 12–13.

40 Jaana Räsänen via email, December 14, 2019. Cf. Tuormala, 2017, pp. 91–93.

41 Cf. Valpola 2015, p. 15.

42 Cf. Valpola 2015, p. 16.

43 Cf. Tuormala 2017, p. 93.

44 Cf. Valpola 2015, p. 17. Cf. http://archinfo.fi/2014/01/paikalliset-ohjelmat/ (last accessed January 8, 2020).

45 Cf. Valpola 2015, p. 18.

46 Cf. Valpola 2011, p. 9.

47 Tiina Valpola, website content from 2009: "The stages of Finnish architectural policy since 1998" via apoli.fi/etusivu (no longer online). Cf. Follow-up Report, 2002.

48 Cf. Valpola 2015, p. 8.

49 Tiina Valpola via email, December 21, 2019. Cf. Salmela 2017, p. 9.
50 Tiina Valpola via email, December 21, 2019.
51 Tiina Valpola via email, December 21, 2019.
52 Cf. https://minedu.fi/en/apoli2020 (last accessed January 10, 2020).
53 Petra Havu in conversation with the author, May 6, 2019.
54 Petra Havu in conversation with the author, May 6, 2019.
55 Cf. "Henkilöt" https://minedu.fi/hanke?tunnus=OKM017:00/2019 (last accessed January 8, 2020).
56 Cf. https://minedu.fi/en/apoli2020 (last accessed January 10, 2020).
57 Cf. Salmela 2017.
58 Cf. https://minedu.fi/en/apoli2020 (last accessed January 10, 2020).
59 Hanna Harris in conversation with the author, May 6, 2019.
60 Cf. Salmela 2017, p. 18.
61 Cf. Salmela 2017, p. 26.
62 Cf. Salmela 2017, p. 26.
63 Cf. Salmela 2017, p. 26.
64 Mikko Hartikainen in conversation with the author, May 7, 2019.
65 Hanna Harris in conversation with the author, May 6, 2019, and Mari Koskinen in conversation with the author, May 7, 2019.
66 Eeva Astala via email, December 4, 2019.
67 Petra Havu in conversation with the author, May 6, 2019.

Architecture as civic education

It is difficult to determine whether the Finnish *Architectural Policy* of 1998 has been able to influence the public awareness of architecture, as these effects are not easily measured. This was also reflected in expert conversations, in which subjective impressions regarding this question diverged widely. Arja-Liisa Kaasinen, head of collaboration and engagement at the Museum of Finnish Architecture in Helsinki, and Riikka Mäkikoskela, executive director of the Finnish Association of Art Schools for Children and Young People, attested that Finnish society has a high level of architecture awareness, although it was not clear whether this had been improved by the *Architectural Policy* or was already the case. As Mäkikoskela said: "In England, as we Finns always say, you can go into a pub and talk about fine arts with anyone—everyone knows about it there. In Finland this would not be possible. But here architecture is part of our general education. Everyone knows about rooms, places, buildings, cities—our environments."[1] Kaasinen confirmed the statement, asserting that the notion of "design and quality for everyone" is a democratic idea that is deeply rooted in Finnish philosophy.[2] Both Mikko Hartikainen of the Finnish National Agency of Education and Henna Haavisto, art teacher at Aurinkolahti Primary School in Vuosaari, are convinced that the architectural policy program has had a positive impact over the past 20 years. While Hartikainen described the general awareness as definitely improved and attributed this to the changes in visual arts education,[3] Haavisto said that "architecture is highly valued. Everyone wants to be an architect. There is also a high awareness that we can influence our built environment and participate in decisions about it. For example, pupils design the rooms they use after school. We involve them in these decisions. They know that they have a lot of say!"[4] Mari Koskinen, competition specialist in the Finnish Association of Architects SAFA, also expressed her decidedly positive opinion: "If you look at how much the newspapers report on architecture, I have to say that architectural awareness has definitely improved. Anyone can be involved now. This is certainly a trend. ... We have a lot of grassroots movements here, groups taking care of empty buildings or organizing events in public spaces. The ways in which people use the city have changed, also how the city looks like. People are interested."[5]

Other interviewees, such as Petra Havu from the Ministry of Education and Culture, were more critical: "Many people didn't understand what I was talking about when I spoke about architectural policy. Many have a very narrow concept of architecture"[6]—an impression shared by Ilpo Vuorela, architecture teacher for children and young people at the Jyväskylä Adult Education Centre. Vuorela acceded that there were good architectural firms and excellent so-called hero-architecture, but everyday architecture is far from owning the label of "high-quality architecture." He added: "For example, I think only about 10% of single-family houses are designed by architects. There are still people who believe that architects would deface their homes. … But it may be that schools and teachers have gradually developed a better awareness of architecture and architecture education. This is great, of course, because it has a direct effect on children and their development."[7] The most critical comment was made by Else Luotinen, a Master's student of architecture and teacher at the newly founded Tiili School of Architecture for Children and Young People in Tampere. She thinks that society's architectural awareness is not well developed: "In my opinion, people do not know their options well enough and are content with what they get, even though they could demand different solutions for the environments in which they live, work, and spend their free time." Luotinen laments that Finland's rural exodus of recent years has led to an abundance of poor-quality buildings in the rapidly growing cities and to the neglect of valuable old buildings in the countryside. According to her, this development will continue until the general awareness of architecture improves and people demand a paradigm shift.[8]

Rather than trying to determine the effects of architectural policy on the public's architectural awareness, it may be more worthwhile to inquire into the ways in which architecture has been promoted as a form of civic education in the past 20 years. Before the following chapters' focus on the implementation of architecture education in the educational system, two individual aspects will be examined in more detail: the establishment of the Architecture Information Centre (Archinfo Finland), which was founded in 2013 and is particularly dedicated to architectural civic education, and the system of architectural competitions, which was reformed in 2012.

Archinfo Finland

The greatest success of the 1998 architectural policy program was undoubtedly the establishment of the Architecture Information Centre Finland—now Archinfo Finland—in 2013, which marked the beginning of the third wave of implementation. Archinfo Finland is a remarkable example showing that it's not mandatory to have huge properties and heavily staffed institutions in order to communicate architecture and improve architectural awareness in society, but that it is possible to achieve great impact with a small number of staff if resources are used wisely, cooperation is established, and results are spread through multipliers.

With the establishment of Archinfo Finland, one of the central demands of the 1998 *Architectural Policy* was fulfilled, namely to identify architecture as a component of art and culture, place it on equal footing with the other arts[9], and thus allow for equal access to the funding policy of the Ministry of Education and Culture.[10] Archinfo Finland is the youngest of a total of eight Art Information Centres, each of which is dedicated to a different artistic field—literature, music, circus, film, dance, theater, and contemporary art.[11] Its main tasks include architectural communication, improving architectural awareness in society, and promoting and advertising Finnish architecture at home and abroad.[12] From the very beginning, the institution has also acted as the single point of contact for the field of architecture education. Archinfo Finland designs projects and concepts for both school and extra-school sectors, as will be described in more detail later, it communicates "best practice" examples and coordinates a network of actors.[13] In addition, Archinfo Finland collects and publishes architectural policies, enables information exchange, offers a networking platform for city and municipal representatives, and sees itself as an initiator of processes and discussions.[14]

Like the other Art Information Centres, Archinfo Finland belongs to the Ministry of Education and Culture and—as its retired founding director Tiina Valpola describes it—receives a significant part of its funding from the ministry: "This includes fundamental work as well as national and international projects, but this must be applied for every year."[15] Although the Art Information Centres are based within the ministry, they are completely independent actors, each working on their own topics in a different way. According to Valpola, Petra Havu of the Ministry of Education and Culture confirmed that although there is an annual meeting with the Art Information Centres, the ministry does not control them. The situation is comparable to the Finnish Cultural and Academic Institutes, of which there are 17 worldwide.[16]

Archinfo Finland is a small informal institution that does not have its own exhibition rooms and employs only four permanent staff members. According to Harris, resources are preferably used in ways that establish cooperation with other organizations. Good networking is ensured by the fact that Archinfo Finland shares an office with the Finnish Association of Architects SAFA, and the Association of Finnish Architects, Offices, and also has a direct relationship with the ministry.

The 1998 *Architectural Policy* and the 2001 report on the status of civic education in architecture, *Discovering*

Architecture, already made apparent that Finland lacked a central institution for bundling communication, facilitating the exchange of different actors, and serving as an advisor, contact point, and information platform.[17] The monitoring group's *Follow-up Report* on the implementation of architectural policy measures, published in 2002, finally called for an "Information and Promotion Centre" for architecture.[18] This was taken up by Paavo Lipponen, the former prime minister, in 2005 in a written interview he gave the magazine *Arkkitehti-lehti* in his capacity as speaker of parliament. He emphasized his demand by saying: "Visibility is needed [for architecture] both in Finland and abroad. We are obliged to do so because there is already a great tradition in this country."[19] When asked why it had taken so long afterwards to establish Archinfo Finland, Tiina Valpola replied: "Simply because nobody believed it could be possible!"[20]

By far the most important milestone regarding the eventual founding of Archinfo Finland was the creation of the special advisor for architecture position in the National Council for Architecture in 2004, which was filled by Tiina Valpola. With her work, Valpola had already anticipated much of Archinfo Finland's thematic focus, as an unpublished lecture from 2011 shows: her tasks at that time not only included the promotion of local and regional architectural policy development and consulting the National Council for Architecture on architectural policy issues—as already described—but also attracting new partners in order to achieve the creation of a better environment, expanding cooperation networks at government and professional levels, and expanding the international network of architectural policy.[21]

The 2012 annual report, which was submitted to the ministry and made available by Valpola, provides information on the two-year foundation procedure. After the possibility of establishing an Architecture Information Centre emerged, preliminary negotiations with the Ministry of Education and Culture began in spring 2011, initiated by the National Council for Architecture. In March 2011, the Committee invited the five key organizations in the sector—the Finnish Association for Architects SAFA, the Association of Finnish Architects' Offices, the Museum of Finnish Architecture, the Alvar Aalto Foundation, and the Building Information Foundation (RTS)—to discuss the collaborative formation of an Architecture Information Centre. After the official statement of intent was signed in April 2011, they entered the national Register of Associations in February 2012. In 2011, as soon as it became apparent that the establishment of an Architecture Information Centre was possible, Valpola, who carried out the practical preparatory work in her capacity as special advisor, hired Jaana Räsänen as an expert in the field of architecture education. Räsänen, who, like Valpola, had until then been a regional level consultant—she had worked as a Regional Artist of Architecture Education in the Uusimaa region—supported Valpola in the two-year preparatory phase for the launch of Archinfo Finland and ensured that architecture education became one of the institution's two central pillars from the very start.[22]

Early in 2013, Archinfo Finland was officially opened as the most recently established of a total of eight Art Information Centres. One of its first activities during this year was the creation of a Finnish-English website that included a database on both architectural policy and on architecture education, which had been set up by Valpola as part of her work as architectural advisor.[23] Since Archinfo Finland needed visibility as a new actor in the cultural and environmental field, events and activities played an important role.

These events were carried out in close cooperation with the five founding institutions, especially the Museum of Finnish Architecture, the Alvar Aalto Foundation, and SAFA. According to Valpola, some of the most important events that took place under her leadership were the national and international architectural policy seminars, which were held in cooperation with the ministries, municipalities, and regions and often combined with activities in the field of architecture education.[24] Participation in the Venice Architecture Biennale and the creation of the *Architecture Navigator*[25] were important steps for the international positioning of Finnish architecture. Among other things, Archinfo Finland also organized press tours for foreign journalists in cooperation with the Alvar Aalto Symposium in Jyväskylä and published a map of Helsinki featuring the most important architectural highlights. Valpola states that the greatest visibility under her direction was achieved during a four-month architectural park event on the Esplanade in Helsinki in 2015, during which two wooden constructions were created that were later exhibited in Venice. The event, which included numerous activities for children and adults, developed into a popular hub and meeting place, attracting around 20,000 visitors.[26]

With the establishment of Archinfo Finland in 2013, the country has acquired a small but powerful institution which has taken the implementation of the *Architectural Policy* into a new phase and continues to be important for civic education in architecture, as will be shown in chapter 5. It is therefore hardly surprising that—when asked why the field of architecture education was so successfully implemented within the 1998 framework of *the Architectural Policy*—Petra Havu of the Ministry of Education and Culture unhesitatingly answered that it was thanks to Tiina Valpola alone. She backed up her statement by saying that she had employed an architecture educator at the very first opportunity in early 2011 to support her in setting up Archinfo Finland. "Architecture education has been so successfully implemented because Tiina Valpola has made it her mission. She has built up the entire organization of the Architecture Information Centre from scratch. She showed the personal commitment to get it up and running."[27] Tiina Valpola answered that same question differently. In her opinion, the 1998 *Architectural Policy* could only have been implemented so successfully because it was a personal concern of then prime minister Paavo Lipponen. "The project would never have reached government level if we hadn't had a prime minister who knew architecture inside out and was actively interested in how the policy process developed."[28] As different as these two assessments are, they nevertheless illustrate that, ultimately, several components must come together to develop and implement a successful architectural policy. Not only do we need committed actors who take up the issue, but it also takes a political climate in which such changes become possible. Just how favorable the political climate must have actually been in Finland during the period in which the *Architectural Policy* was developed and implemented can be deduced from an article in the magazine *Arkkitehti-lehti* in 2005, in which former prime minister Paavo Lipponen, who was speaker of parliament at the time, was asked about the significance of the 1998 *Architectural Policy* and listed architecture as one of his most important hobbies.[29]

ARCHINFO
HELSINKI
ARCHITECTURAL HIGHLIGHTS
SPECIAL EDITION:
HELSINKI
BUILT THROUGH
COMPETITIONS
HOW ARCHITECTURAL COMPETITIONS
HAVE SHAPED THE CITY
FOR MORE FINNISH ARCHITECTURE
EXPLORE THE ONLINE NAVIGATOR
NAVI.FINNISHARCHITECTURE.FI

Fig. 14

Architecture competitions as civic education

The Finnish Association of Architects SAFA is one of the most important actors in Finland with respect to the development of the *Architectural Policy* and its implementation. It has shown a particular commitment to architectural civic education and architecture education for children and young people. The association not only acts as a promoter of numerous educational projects but has played an active role from the very beginning. SAFA has organized conferences and trainings, developed and promoted teaching materials, and—until the establishment of Archinfo Finland—acted as an information interface in the field. It is worth noting that SAFA also contributes to improving architectural civic education in society in its role as chief supervisor, consultant, and co-arranger of architectural competitions.[30] In the Finnish *Architectural Policy* of 1998, architectural competitions are characterized as a central instrument for promoting quality and innovation in the building sector. Moreover, they are "a form of further education and a way of opening up opportunities for young architects. The large number of alternative solutions ... facilitates the public debate about best options for the environment."[31] SAFA's pride in the Finnish competition tradition of which it has been a part for over 100 years is also shown by the city map *Helsinki Built Through Competitions. How Architectural Competitions have Shaped the City,* which SAFA published on the occasion of its 125th anniversary in 2017 and in cooperation with Archinfo Finland.[32] The map presents 100 "architectural highlights" of the city built as a result of architectural competitions between 1863 and 2017. (Fig. 14) Mari Koskinen, who works as a competition expert for SAFA, pointed out in a personal conversation that it would be difficult to re-establish such a system at present. The principle only works today because both clients and planners have already become used to it. Nowadays everyone tends to be more control-oriented. According to Koskinen, developers want a "soft process" and prefer to work with people they already know. In a competition, however, you have less control—you don't know who is participating and who is winning; all you know is that you are getting the best possible result. Competitions are also highly valued in Finland because "almost every big name in Finnish architecture has had their breakthrough through a competition. And many of them were very young at the time."[33]

One of the peculiarities of the Finnish competition system is that in most of the procedures since 2012, submissions have been made available to the public via the internet. The fact that competition entries are exhibited is not a distinct feature but is, for example, also stipulated by the guidelines for German planning competitions.[34] Yet in Germany these presentations usually take place only after the jury has made its decision. In Finland, however, the entries are made available to the public before the expert jury has had the chance to view the plans. The participating architectural offices agree that their entries will be made available to the public on the competition website and that the feedback will be used as input for the evaluation.[35] In conversation with the author, Mari Koskinen—competition specialist at SAFA—has shed light on this exceptional procedure and the importance of the Finnish competition system. "When I started working for SAFA seven years ago, it was new that all submissions were displayed on the internet. Of course, we'd had physical exhibitions in the past, but having them online was new. We had to think about how it could be done and how it would affect the evaluation process. And then it finally became standard. The way people can interact varies a bit from competition to competition. Sometimes it's just an image that you see. Sometimes you can comment on it, sometimes you can 'like' it, as on Facebook."[36] However, Koskinen notes, the procedure does not have a direct influence on the decision-making process, which is why there is also some criticism about the process: "We only collect the information and present it to the jury. The jury can then decide whether or not to include the comments or results in the evaluation process."[37] In her opinion, the audience vote has little influence on the jury. Rather, it is an opportunity for the jury to gauge what people think: "It's not a professional evaluation—maybe people just liked the picture because it showed a nice summer day. The jury makes the professional evaluation." Koskinen is aware that this appears to be contradictory: "I know that sounds contradictory. On the one hand, we let people make their comments, and then we don't take them into account in the evaluation process. But the door is opened for public opinion to be heard." In the end, according to Koskinen, it is necessary that experts make the decisions, as only they can judge what is spatially, architecturally, and functionally appropriate and how a project will affect the neighborhood. While it may be quite possible that the political representatives on the jury are more influenced by public opinion, the decision will of course be based on the evaluation criteria. Asked whether this procedure did actually cause discontent among citizens—giving them the impression that their opinion was only being asked for formally—Koskinen replied that the overall effect has been positive even if, ultimately, the public discussion only minimally influences the jury's decision: "The citizens have a lot of say in our planning processes. It

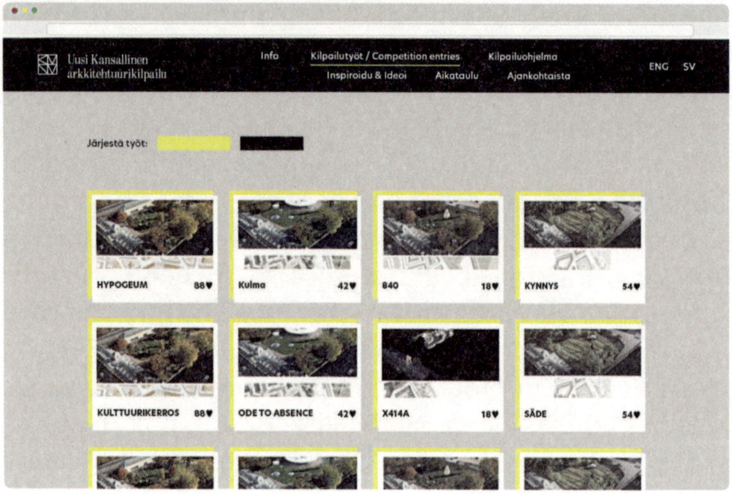

Fig. 15

is important that they are invited to give feedback. This is an important way of communicating with them, and it can help them feel more involved after the process is over. It's a kind of psychological thinking." According to Koskinen, it is part of the Finnish mentality that things must be transparent. In the end, it is not necessarily a question of actually influencing the jury, but rather that it's the organizers' duty to let citizens know what's going on.[38]

Koskinen explained the importance of sharing this information by the example of the "Europan 14" competition in 2017, which Europan Finland organized in cooperation with the City Planning Department of Helsinki.[39] Before the competition was announced, residents were invited to a public event in order to express their position, wishes, or fears. These were then included in the tender, and there were many negative votes. The project involved a section of motorway that was to be converted into a regular road. Those affected assumed that it would not work and would

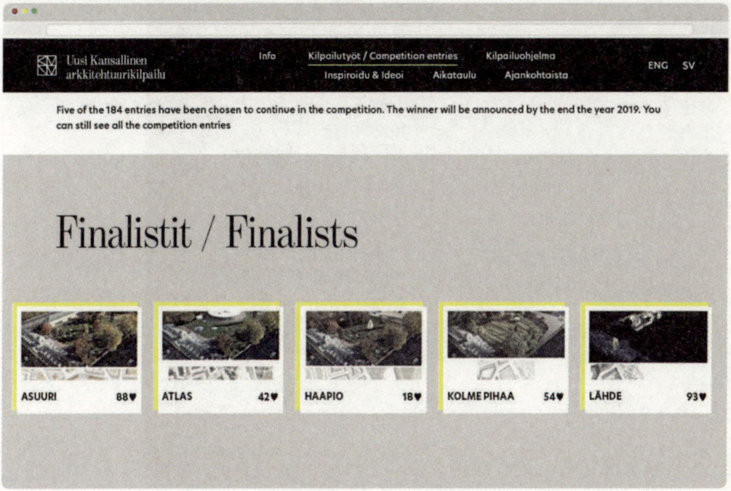

Fig. 16

cause traffic jams and expressed their rejection accordingly. When the entries were presented after the competition, about 40 residents came to see the results. The mood was now quite different when they saw how the plan could be made to work. They no longer said that it was wrong and would not work, but started to think through the plans. For example, they wondered whether there would be enough winter storage space for boats. It was suddenly so concrete. The change of mood had come about "because the images existed, and they saw that a transformation was actually possible. And they saw that their concerns were taken seriously. They were no longer categorically against it but were now part of the process. And when the results were finally published, they were really happy about the winner. It was one of the contributions in which forest was preserved, which was important for the local residents. ... We learned that people can be very much against a planning process if they are not involved."[40]

Fig. 17

Mari Koskinen could not quantify how many people actually look at the competition entries on the internet. She reported a high level of participation in the case of the "New National," the most prominent ongoing competition at the time of the conversation, which involved the extension to the Finnish National Museum designed by Eliel Saarinen. There were urban activist groups, for example, that were very committed to urban planning and development: "They have social media channels where they discuss everything. That's trendy here. I know that these people discuss certain contributions in their groups and illustrate what advantages or disadvantages this or that design would bring. But they are aware that everything they discuss is independent from the jury process." In any case, it could be said that architectural competitions were a topic of public interest and that public procedures certainly contributed to improving the awareness of architecture.[41]

The online presentation of the competition for the "New National," which Koskinen described in conversation as a particularly good example, shows how such a competition presentation is organized. The tender text of the competition contains precise information about the system layout of the two PDF posters that could be submitted: it specified exactly where certain images, photos, texts, or floor plans were to be placed and what format they were to be given. That way, maximum comparability of the contributions is guaranteed. Models are not envisaged for either the first or the second phase of the competition.[42]

The competition website confirms Koskinen's observations. A total of 15,634 audience votes were cast for the 184 entries. (Fig. 15) However, none of the audience favorites such as "Hypogeum," "Kulma," or "Maija," which received between 1,045 and 882 votes, are among the finalists selected by the jury for the first round of the second competition phase. (Fig. 16) These were in the middle to lower field of the audience ranking with 93 to 18 points and received a total of only 303 votes, which is less than 2% of the total of 15,634 votes. The recently selected work in first place, "Atlas," (Fig. 17) which was submitted by JKMM Architects—the office that has caused a sensation in recent years with projects such as the Amos Rex, the Think Corner and the Harald Herlin Learning Centre (referenced earlier) and which is currently one of the most acclaimed Finnish offices—only received 42 audience votes. In the end, the audience favorite "Hypogeum" at least received a "commendatory recognition."

It is remarkable that neither the reformed competition system nor the founding of Archinfo Finland—which can justifiably be considered the greatest success of Finnish *Architectural Policy*—were explicitly mentioned in the expert discussions as either a success or consequence of the *Architectural Policy*. This is apparently because—from a Finnish perspective—the time gap of 14 or 15 years is too long to make those direct connections discernible that appear obvious from the outside.

Conclusion: Civic education in Baukultur

Germany could learn a lot from Finland with regard to how the general awareness of Baukultur in society could be improved. The prerequisite for this, however, would be to first formulate a lack in this respect, meaning the official acknowledgement that this area is in need of action and improvement. It is noteworthy that studies such as *Bildungsorte und Lernwelten der Baukultur* (Educational Venues and Learning Worlds of Baukultur),[43] recently published by the Wüstenrot Stiftung, or the *Bildungsplattform*,[44] also published by the Federal Foundation of Baukultur in November 2019, tend to give the impression that Baukultur education in Germany is well established and that there is no need for improvement.

Moreover, Germany can learn from Finland that it requires neither heavily staffed and large institutions nor grand exhibition spaces in order to foster a public awareness of Baukultur. The establishment of an architecture information center, which would help to enhance the position of architecture in the public eye and its status in society, would be desirable and could effectively support the work of the Federal Foundation of Baukultur. For one, the Finnish example shows that such an institution does not need a fixed location in the analog world but can find a home on the internet. On the other hand, it becomes apparent that—with clever strategies designed to use and strengthen existing resources—it is possible to achieve a great deal with a relatively small number of staff. It also seems sensible to concentrate on three priorities: architectural communication, architectural policy, and architecture education.

Finnish competition policy, in which the contributions are presented to the public in advance and through which public discussion is invited before the expert jury begins its work, would also be a promising method to promote architectural awareness and interest in Germany. What at first glance appears to be a radical step, on closer inspection proves to be less radical and yet efficient. The skepticism among experts as to whether the "average citizen" should or must be included in the selection process of competition procedures is probably at a similar level in Germany and Finland. However, the Finnish example shows that it is quite possible to involve citizens in the decision-making process at an early stage and make it transparent without granting them real decision-making powers. The effects are nevertheless positive, as the Finnish example shows.

1 Riikka Mäkikoskela in conversation with the author, May 13, 2019.
2 Arja-Liisa Kaasinen in conversation with the author, May 13, 2019.
3 Mikko Hartikainen in conversation with the author, May 7, 2019.
4 Henna Haavisto in conversation with the author, May 10, 2019.
5 Mari Koskinen in conversation with the author, May 7, 2019.
6 Petra Havu in conversation with the author, May 6, 2019.
7 Ilpo Vuorela via email, June 15, 2019.
8 Else Luotinen via email, December 3, 2019.
9 Cf. Architectural policy 1999, p. 15.
10 Tiina Valpola via email, December 19, 2019.
11 Cf. www.lastenkulttuuri.fi/en/childrens-culture-finland/art-information-centres (accessed January 3, 2020).
12 Hanna Harris in conversation with the author, May 6, 2019. Cf. also: archinfo.fi/en (accessed January 3, 2020).
13 Cf. archinfo.fi/en/architecture-education (accessed January 3, 2020).
14 Cf. archinfo.fi/en/architecture-policy (accessed January 3, 2020).
15 Tiina Valpola via email, December 15, 2019.
16 Cf. instituutit.fi/en/info (accessed January 3, 2020).
17 Cf. Architectural policy 1999, pp. 24–25, and Korpelainen and Yanar 2001, p. 40.
18 Cf. Follow-up Report 2002, p. 27.
19 Hautajärvim 2005, p. 20.
20 Tiina Valpola in phone conversation, December 15, 2019.
21 Cf. Valpola 2011, p. 16.
22 Jaana Räsänen via email, November 27, 2019.
23 Cf. Arkkitehtuurin tiedotuskeskuksen /Arkkitehtuurikeskus ry:n vuoden 2013 toimintakertomus (Archinfo Finland activity report 2013), pp. 5–6.
24 Tiina Valpola via email, January 3, 2020.
25 C. http://www.finnisharchitecture.fi/ (accessed January 15, 2020).
26 Tiina Valpola via email, January 3, 2020; also cf. archinfo.fi/en/2015/06/the-re-creation-installation-transforms-the-esplanade-park-into-a-hotspot-of-architecture-related-activities/ (accessed January 12, 2020).
27 Petra Havu in conversation with the author, May 6, 2019.
28 Tiina Valpola in conversation with the author, May 8, 2019. Paavo Lipponen was prime minister from 1995 until 2003.
29 Cf. Hautajärvim 2005, pp. 20–21.
30 Cf. www.finnisharchitecture.fi/finnish-association-of-architects-safa *and* www.safa.fi/en/architectural-competitions-in-finland (accessed January 1, 2020).
31 Cf. Architectural policy 1999, p. 24.
32 Cf. www.finnisharchitecture.fi/finnish-association-of-architects-safa *and* www.safa.fi/en/architectural-competitions-in-finland (accessed January 1, 2020).
33 Mari Koskinen in conversation with the author, May 7, 2019. Cf. also: Nikula 2000, pp. 88–89.
34 Cf. Richtlinien für Planungswettbewerbe RPW 2013, p. 9, www.bak.de/w/files/bak/03berufspraxis/hoaivergabe/rpw_2013.pdf (accessed January 3, 2020).
35 Cf. Competition brief "New National" 2018, p. 8.
36 Mari Koskinen in conversation with the author, May 7, 2019.
37 Mari Koskinen in conversation with the author, May 7, 2019.
38 Mari Koskinen in conversation with the author, May 7, 2019.
39 Cf. www.europan.fi/archive/#modal=/site/suburban-boulevard (accessed January 3, 2020).
40 Mari Koskinen in conversation with the author, May 7, 2019.
41 Mari Koskinen in conversation with the author, May 7, 2019.
42 Cf. Competition brief "New National" 2018, p. 31.
43 Wüstenrot Stiftung 2019.
44 Cf. www.bundesstiftung-baukultur.de/netzwerk/bildung (accessed January 3, 2020).

Architecture in the Finnish educational system

As mentioned earlier, the overwhelmingly positive accounts of the 1998 *Architectural Policy* and its implementation of architecture education in the educational system caused quite a stir in Germany. The basis for this was *Discovering Architecture. Civic Education in Architecture in Finland*, a report published by the Finnish Association of Architects SAFA in 2001. During an afternoon seminar on the subject organized by the SAFA Research and Training Committee in November 1999, it had become clear that the participants were all confronted with the same problems: a lack of contact with other colleagues or institutions, a lack of teaching materials, and a lack of opportunities for further training. As none of the participants had a clear overview of what was being offered at that time with respect to Finland's civic education in architecture, it was clear that further investigation would be necessary.[1] As part of the study, which was published in 2001 and financed by the National Council for Architecture, the authors Heini Korpelainen and Anu Yanar gathered information about 140 projects in 45 cities and learned about another 60 projects.[2] According to Tiina Valpola, during the first "enthusiastic phase" immediately after the publication of the 1998 *Architectural Policy*, there arose a wealth of projects made possible by the funding policy of the Ministry of Education and the National Council for Architecture.[3] In the account, the authors reported on the first three lower or upper secondary schools in which architecture had been integrated into the subjects of art, geography, history, mathematics, or religion.[4] However, the most cited milestone in the integration of architecture education in schools is the year 2003, when architecture was integrated as a separate topic of visual arts teaching in lower and upper secondary schools.[5]

Architecture education in the regular school system

When asked whether architecture education was well established in the Finnish school system, almost all the experts interviewed answered that there is still a high demand in this field. The current *National Core Curricula for Basic Education* and *Upper Secondary Education*, both of which came into force in 2016, revealed that architecture is less present in the curricula for basic education, as the nine-year common school is called, and for general upper secondary schools, or grammar schools, than would be expected. In comparison to the previous curricula, which came into force for basic education in 2004 and for upper secondary education in 2003, it can be seen that the tendency is even in decline and that much less architecture education is being provided today. For example, the module "Environmental Aesthetics, Architecture, and Design," which was part of the basic education curriculum of 2004 for the subject of art, has been deleted in the new curriculum. The module provided for students to explore and document their natural and built environment, architecture, and built heritage. In addition, they were to learn to read and design 3D objects, plans, and true-to-scale models.[6] While the old curriculum still explicitly mentioned the individual art disciplines, the new *National Core Curriculum for Basic Education* only mentions the keyword "architecture" in connection with religious education for grades 3-6. Here it is intended that students should also deal with church architecture.[7] Somewhat more frequently, altogether eleven times, the keyword "built environment" is mentioned. In the first two grades, built environments and cultural heritage will be dealt with in crafts,[8] in history—which will be taught from the 3rd grade onwards[9]—and in geography, which is on the curriculum from the 7th grade onwards.[10] However, these topics are primarily anchored in environmental studies,[11] a multidisciplinary subject which—according to the *National Core Curriculum for Basic Education*—comprises the knowledge fields biology, geography, physics and health education, includes a sustainability aspect, and brings together perspectives from the natural and social sciences. Environmental studies is taught in grades 1-6 and is most comparable to the German subject Sachkunde, which is taught in primary school. Among other things, the aim is to encourage pupils to get to know and understand the natural and built environment.[12] Surprisingly, the *National Core Curriculum for Basic Education* does not explicitly mention architecture or built environment education in the context of visual arts. Only one of the three compulsory courses, covering

"Formed and built environments (KU2)" in the curriculum for upper secondary education, Secondary Level II, explicitly refers to architecture and built environment education.[13] Furthermore, architecture and built environments are only mentioned here in connection with church buildings in the subject religion, and in the subjects geography and health education.[14]

Yet, according to Mikko Hartikainen of the Finnish National Agency of Education, when the text of the *National Core Curriculum for Basic Education 2014* is closely examined, the fact that the explicit architectural terminology is less present in the new core curriculum than in the previous one does not mean that there shouldn't be any more architecture education. On the contrary, Hartikainen claims it is one of the key contents in the content area covering visual culture in the environment in visual arts education. Design, architecture, and built environment are primarily examined and provided for in the subjects visual arts and crafts.[15] "Loopholes" for architecture education are probably hidden behind the regularly recurring formulation "and other forms of visual culture."[16] It is noteworthy that according to both curricula, pupils are to be encouraged to influence their environment and society within the framework of visual arts.[17] At the same time, the keywords "participation, involvement, and creating a sustainable environment" are among the overarching competencies that are promoted in the Finnish school system from year one and that form the basis of all subjects.[18] For example, under point T7 of the "Transversal Competencies" it states that, for level 1-2, "participation is the basic prerequisite for effective democracy. Skills in participation and involvement as well as a responsible awareness of the future can only be learned through practice. The school environment provides a protected framework for this, while Basic Education provides the basis for pupils to grow into active citizens who use their democratic rights and freedoms responsibly."[19] Pupils should also be explicitly involved in the design of the learning environment, which plays an important role in the principles of the curricula.[20]

According to Mikko Hartikainen, it is impossible to tell from the *National Core Curriculum* how much architecture or built environment education is actually offered, because decisions on the content of courses covering the concrete built environment are ultimately made by local education providers, and therefore the selection of contents varies as a result of decisions made on the basis of the requirements of local curricula, annual school plans, and the varied pedagogical approaches and methods of teachers. However, more and more educational providers and schools are making good use of the opportunities provided for in their respective local cultural education plans to strengthen, for example, architecture education.[21] These plans are drawn up by municipalities in cooperation with local and regional artistic and cultural institutions and other stakeholders. Thus, networking with extracurricular venues and experts is ensured, and it is guaranteed that each region can center its own cultural heritage and that all pre-school and community school pupils have access to culture and the arts each year.[22] It is precisely at this point that local architectural policies finally come into play, which, as Jaana Räsänen explains in the guest article of this publication, all refer to the topic of architecture education.

This explains why the two *National Core Curricula* are relatively insignificant and why learning goals and contents are formulated with utmost openness. Even the exact distribution of lessons, which is regulated in "Government Decree 422/2012," is ultimately in the hands of local educational institutions. One example would be the distribution of lessons set by the city of Kuopio for the nine-year basic school. (Fig. 18) As Mikko Hartikainen explains, a total of 41 hours per week for grades 1-6 each year and 21 hours per week in grades 7-9 each year are allocated for the so-called arts and skills subject group, which consists of visual arts, music, crafts, physical education, and home economics. Accordingly, in the nine years of common school a total of 62 hours per week must be taken in that subject group each year, whereby an hour per week corresponds to 38 lessons of each 45 minutes each year.[23] The distribution plan of the city of Kuopio shows that almost one third of those 62 hours per week, 20 in total, are devoted to physical education. Added to this are the three compulsory hours for home economics in the 7th grade. The compulsory lessons for music (8 hours), visual arts (9 hours) and crafts (14 hours) are distributed in such a way that there are compulsory lessons in all three subjects throughout grades 1 to 7. There are two hours per week for crafts and one for visual arts and music each—though in the 4th grade in visual arts and in the 7th grade the compulsory lessons in both subjects increase to two. In addition, a total of eight elective courses are scheduled, in which students may choose from the entire spectrum of the five subjects. Three of these are in grades 1-6, with one lesson in the 3rd and two in the 4th grade. Five more, three in the 8th and two in the 9th grade, are allotted to so-called lower secondary education.[24] Theoretically, it is therefore possible that pupils won't have any arts classes after the 7th grade, as it is no longer compulsory from then on.

As the city of Kuopio was already pursuing the goal of improving architecture education in schools, kindergartens, and vocational training under measure 16 of its first local architectural policy in 2007[25]—this goal also being renewed in the second architectural policy of 2017[26]—it can be assumed that the topics architecture and built environment will certainly play a role in the context of visual arts or crafts lessons. That schools are also seeking to collaborate with external partners or institutions in order to teach building culture was also evident from discussions with the founders of the two architecture schools for children. Pihla Meskanen, founder of ARKKI, reported that her school collaborates with Helsinki's neighboring cities of Espoo and Vantaa within the framework of the cultural education plan. According to Meskanen, both cities have been paying ARKKI in the last five years of collaboration, which is ultimately free of charge for the schools. Mervi Eskelinen, director of the Lastu School in Lapinlahti, also mentioned a collaboration with an upper secondary school in Lapinlahti, which will occur regularly if enough students register. Her description of the scope of these courses shows how flexible the system of weekly working hours can be: "The school year is divided into five phase, and we teach one of them, so that we have about five hours of lessons per week."[27] Therefore, if the distribution plan for one form stipulates one hour of visual arts per week, this does not mean that the pupils have art lessons once a week for 45 minutes, but that the lessons can be clustered—similar to the so-called epoch teaching of Waldorf schools for example—so that more intensive work is possible.

Although, at first glance, it seems as if architecture education has been cut back as part of the new *National Core Curriculum for Basic Education*, it became clear in discussions with Hanna Harris, Lotta Leskelä, Jaana Räsänen, Pihla Meskanen, and Mervi Eskelinen that the new curriculum also creates a potential for architecture education via its reference to the newly created "multidisciplinary

Distribution of classroom hours: Basic education

Subject/class	1	2	3	4	5	6	7	8	9	1-9
Mothertongue and literature	7	7	5	5	4	4	3	4	3	42
A1-language			2	2	3	2	2	2	3	16
B1-language						2	2	1	1	6
Mathematics	3	3	3	4	4	4	3	4	4	32
Environmental studies	2	2	2	2	3	3				14
Biology and geography							2	2	3	7
Physics and Chemistry							2	2	3	7
Health Education							0,5	1,5	1	3
Religion/Ethics	1	1	2	1	1	1	1	1	1	10
History and social studies				1	2	2	2	2	3	12
Music	1	1	1	1	1	1	2			8
Visual Art	1	1	1	2	1	1	2			9
Crafts	2	2	2	2	2	2	2			14
Physical Education	2	2	3	2	2	2	2	3	2	20
Home economics							3			3
Artistic and practical elective subjects			1	2				3	2	8
Guidance Counseling							0,5	0,5	1	2
Elective subjects					2	1		3	3	9
Kuopio bonus hours	1	1	1							3
Lessons per week	20	20	23	24	25	25	29	29	30	225
Optional language				2	2	2	2	(2)	(2)	8

Fig. 18

learning modules." These offer "excellent opportunities ... for cooperations between the school and the society around it."[28] For example, Pihla Meskanen reported on a cooperation with a school in Central Finland that wanted to establish architecture as a subject. "They interpreted the new curriculum as a way to offer different electives. We then developed a curriculum with them and in the first year we had an architect there for four hours a week. Now, the teachers use the jointly developed material in order to continue the lessons on their own." A similar project is currently being managed by ARKKI at a school in Helsinki. This government-sponsored project is taking place in three classes. "Every Friday, architects come to class and work with the teachers all day. In relation to the school curriculum, the ARKKI-led, phenomenon-based program combines different topics in a multidisciplinary manner through architecture."[29] Furthermore, as Räsänen notes, the curriculum encourages the use of all kinds of surroundings as learning environments.[30] Thus, according to the curriculum for basic education, not only the interior and exterior of the school should be used, but also nature and the built environment,[31] which in turn offers new possibilities for architecture education.[32]

Generally, architecture seems to be quite present in schools even without explicit mention in the *National Core Curricula*. This may be because—at least in the last 20 years since the 1998 *Architectural Policy* —architecture has started to take on a relatively self-evident role within arts education. However, it may also be because architecture and architectural history have traditionally been well anchored in Finnish teacher education due to their outstanding importance for the nation-building process. Riikka Mäkikoskela, executive director of the Finnish Association of Art Schools for Children and Young People, reported that the Art History

Faculty at the University of Helsinki has a strong focus on the history of architecture: "Students sometimes complain that they mainly study architectural history and the history of fine arts."[33] Henna Haavisto, who works as an art teacher at the Aurinkolahti Primary School in Vuosaari and studied at Aalto University in Espoo, confirmed the high percentage of architectural history in her study program. She claims that she learned the most about the city and architecture in a seminar on environmental education, which was a compulsory course in teacher training called "Space and Environment": "We studied in Helsinki City a lot, we looked at architecture and had lectures on how and by whom Helsinki's architecture was built, and went through different times and styles. It was a bigger course, a four-credit course, I think. There were excursions, and we got to know different rooms, buildings, and some architects who talked about their projects, but we were also introduced to the most important laws that you have to know when it comes to architecture."[34] And Lotta Leskelä, curator of education at the Alvar Aalto Museum in Jyväskylä, who trained at the University of Lapland in Rovaniemi stated that she studied architectural history as part of art history courses too, but she attended also some courses in architecture education and environmental education.[35]

Mikko Hartikainen from the Finnish National Agency of Education also stressed that art teacher training in Finland has traditionally always been broadly structured. It is less about "fine arts" training but rather "visual culture education." In this context, environmental education, for example, has played a prominent role since the late 1960s and early 1970s, and as Pirkko Pohjakallio-Koskinen describes in her 2010 article "Mapping Environmental Education Approaches in Finnish Art Education," it has undergone various changes since 1970.[36]

One of the surprises that the examination of the Finnish school system has revealed in relation to architecture education is the realization that arts education is less present in the Finnish school system than is generally assumed. Indeed, the Finnish school system today has the reputation of having an exceptionally high proportion of arts lessons, since there is no other subject in which learning and creative thinking—key educational goals in Finnish education—could be more effectively learned. Riikka Mäkikoskela, executive director of the Finnish Association of Art Schools for Children and Young People, confirmed that this was certainly still the case in the 1980s and 1990s, although there had already been a massive wave of cutbacks in the 1970s. In the course of the 2000s, however, this changed so massively that Mäkikoskela describes it as a veritable "cleaning out of art" over the past 20 years. Under the conservative government, a paradigm shift in favor of the economy has taken place, which she believes will be reflected in society within the next ten years, since the arts system collapses quickly if it is not maintained.[37] What is surprising is not only the relatively low number of only nine hours of compulsory lessons—as shown by the city of Kuopio's timetable—but especially the fact that students usually do not come into contact with trained art teachers until their 7th grade, at the age of 12 to 13, which is exactly the moment when they usually drop out, lose interest, and are difficult to motivate. Yet in the first six years of school, arts lessons are usually taken over by class teachers who are relatively insufficiently trained for this, as Henna Haavisto and Riikka Mäkikoskela pointed out.[38] As the Kuopio city timetable shows, it is thus possible that pupils who drop art classes after 7th grade have only been taught by trained art teachers for a single year of their schooling, which is very little.

Professor Martti Raevaara, head of the Master's degree program in art education and head of the Faculty of Art, explained how Aalto University is trying to counteract this unfortunate state of affairs: "Aalto University cooperates with the class teacher degree programmes of different universities, so that students from there can apply to Aalto University for a minor course of study and complete 60 credits, i.e. one academic year. Most of the students come from the University of Helsinki, but some come from other universities too. We have annually a large number of applicants, but unfortunately we can take only three to five of them to full-time minor studies at Aalto University. That's why we have a special agreement with the University of Tampere to implement the minor studies of art education in collaboration for 12 students in Tampere. So, we have a total of about 15 to 18 minor students every year, who take art education subject studies of 60 credits during one study year. We don't really get much extra resources for this—but we want to help in this situation because there are more and more class teachers having very little studies in art education, and only few with this 60 credits minor. It is little, but at least it is something. The University of Lapland also accepts five to six minor students a year."[39]

The fact that arts education and architecture education nevertheless have the reputation of having a large presence in the Finnish school system could ultimately also be due to a misunderstanding. The difference between the *National Core Curriculum for Basic Education* and the *National Core Curriculum for Basic Education in the Arts* is not necessarily immediately obvious to outsiders. Both have a similar name, both are published by the Finnish National Agency for Education, and visually differ only by a slightly different shade of blue. In terms of content, however, they are two completely different curricula. While one relates to the nine-year common school, Basic Education in the Arts is an extracurricular curriculum in which the content for private or state-supported arts and music schools is regulated.

Architecture education in Basic Education in the Arts

Basic Education in the Arts is a singularly Finnish specialty. It offers children and young people extra-curricular arts and music lessons, which—following the example of youth music school lessons—are taught on a long-term basis and systematically progress from level to level.[40] Basic Education in the Arts has its roots in the early 1970s: in the course of reforming the school system from a two-tier system to a nine-year common school, arts instruction was for the first time subjected to massive cuts in the curriculum. This led to considerable protests in society.[41] Through grassroots movements, parents, teachers, and artists all over Finland joined forces and founded municipal and private arts schools with the aim of absorbing cuts to the afternoon program and ensuring continuous, sequential arts lessons comparable to those in youth music schools.[42] As Elisse Heinimaa notes, the Finnish Association of Art Schools for Children and Young People was founded in 1982 after an experimental start-up phase and as a community of interest. As its overarching goal, it stipulated that arts schools should not be seen as institutions preparing for artistic professions, but should benefit all children and young people and be more conducive to general personality development.[43] In 1992, as Mikko Hartikainen describes the development, the first law concerning Basic Education in the Arts was passed, which was intended to encourage communities to expand the offer of extracurricular arts education. This was followed in 1993 by the first *National Core Curriculum for Basic Education in the Arts*, published by the National Board of Education (now the Finnish National Agency for Education). After the act was revised in 1998, the curriculum was also adapted in 2000. From then on, it defined two curricula, a *general* and an *advanced syllabus*, which differ in terms of teaching scope. For example, the *general program* is based on 500 teaching units and the *advanced program* on 1,300 hours.[44] Since 2005, Basic Education in the Arts has included nine arts disciplines—visual arts, crafts, media arts, music, literature, circus, dance, theatre, and architecture—for which the Finnish National Agency of Education has drawn up two respective curricula, *general* and *advanced*.

One of the overarching goals formulated for architecture in the two curricula is to build a lifelong relationship with architecture. In addition, the aim is to foster conditions for individual expression and interpretation. "Architecture will be explored experimentally as spatial art and as omnipresent built environment, ranging from individual artefacts to extensive units." Moreover, the lessons are intended to familiarize students with environmental planning and design processes but also with the maintenance and renewal of cultural heritage in the context of sustainable development.[45] The program begins in early childhood education with a playful exploration of one's own living environment and introduces planning, design, and three-dimensional work. The pre-school courses comprise not only individual work but also group work, so that even the youngest children already have the chance to learn to include and consider other positions.[46]

The *general syllabus* aims to encourage children and young people to develop a relationship with architecture, introduce pupils to the multifaceted and multi-sensory perception of their environment, and help them develop an understanding of the interaction between humans, nature, and the built environment. But the aim is also to achieve "built environment literacy," i.e. to assist children and young people in learning to read and make sense of the built environment. For this, the basics of architectural history, cultural heritage, and contemporary architecture are taught. Furthermore, architecture is to be experienced as a field between art and science and in its relationship to the other arts. The pupils are to be introduced to planning and design processes, as well as made familiar with their potential for exerting influence.[47]

While the *general syllabus* estimates a total of 500 hours per week of 45 minutes each—with 300 hours for the "common" component and 200 hours for the *thematic studies* part in which an in-depth study takes place—the *advanced syllabus* estimates a total of 1,300 hours per week. From these, 800 are so-called core studies and 500 hours are specialized studies.[48] The descriptions of the contents and goals of the two curricula hardly differ and usually only provide for a more active learner's part in the *advanced syllabus*. For example, the *thematic studies in architecture* sections in the *general syllabus* are intended to "encourage" pupils to engage with the history of architecture, built heritage, and contemporary architecture, and to improve their general knowledge in the field.[49] In comparison, the *advanced syllabus* animates pupils to "undertake extensive research in the history of architecture, built heritage and contemporary architecture."[50] While the *general syllabus* is intended to "guide students to develop their architectural thinking and to understand key concepts," the *advanced syllabus* has been designed to encourage students to "deepen their skills and develop architectural ideas and solutions."[51]

Within the framework of Basic Education in the Arts, architecture is taught mainly in two schools of architecture for children and young people: ARKKI, School of Architecture for Children and Youth—which was founded by Pihla Meskanen in 1993 and operates in Helsinki, Espoo, and Vantaa—and Lastu School for Architecture and Environmental Culture in Lapinlahti in Central Finland, founded by Mervi Eskelinen. According to Riikka Mäkikoskela, executive director of the Finnish Association of Art Schools for Children and Young People, at least four visual arts schools under the association also offer the basic program in architecture in addition to the specialized architecture schools for children and young people. One of the first schools to offer an architecture program since 1996 is the Visual Art School Jyväskylä, which has been operating as an independent unit under the umbrella of the Jyväskylä Adult Education Centre since 2016.[52] According to Ilpo Vuorela, who has taught architecture in Jyväskylä since 1998, it is the only institution besides ARKKI to offer the Basic Education in the Arts *advanced syllabus* in architecture. The school has 45 to 50 students per year in the field of architecture and, as Vuorela pointed out, offers teaching more or less exclusively in the context of Basic Education in the Arts. Short-term courses, summer workshops, or cooperation with schools or the Jyväskylä-based Alvar Aalto Foundation only rarely take place.[53]

Although architecture is only a small branch of the Basic Education in the Arts program, Mäkikoskela pointed out that architecture courses are often offered at visual arts schools, as they can easily be integrated into the curricula for visual arts or crafts in the context of Basic Education in the Arts. Architecture courses are also popular because, like media or photography courses, they particularly appeal to boys, who are severely underrepresented in Basic Education in the Arts.[54] Around 80% of pupils in the program are girls, as shown in the 2017 *Compendium Cultural Policies and Trends in Europe*.[55]

It can be assumed that the system of Basic Education in the Arts, in which architecture is on equal footing with the other eight arts, as well as the now famous architecture schools for children and young people, have made a significant contribution to the ways in which Finland is perceived—and rightly so—as the undisputed pioneer in the field of architecture education. However, a presentation by the director of the Association of Basic Education in the Arts, Anu Hietala, on January 26, 2017 at the LKCA Conference in Utrecht shows how small the field of architecture within Basic Education in the Arts actually is. Hietala reports on a total of 393 art and music schools in Finland (including 120 Adult Education Centres), located in 251 municipalities, which represents 85% of all Finnish municipalities. They are attended by almost 130,000 pupils, which is only about 15% of a cohort[56]—which seems to be a relatively generous estimate, as Mikko Hartikainen's estimates are only around 11-14% of a cohort.[57] Hietala's summary table shows how small the proportion of students in architecture programs is. With 69,317 participants, more than half of the total of 129,218 students enrolled are studying music, followed by 29,943 in dance, and 17,473 in the visual arts. With 408 students, architecture is a niche field, which is only undercut by 74 participants in media art.[58] This means that only 0.32% of students participating in the Basic Education in the Arts program actually choose architecture.

According to Mäkikoskela, the relatively small reach of Basic Education in the Arts in Finland also means that the program is not without controversy. One of the criticisms might be that it reaches only a small percentage of children and young people in a given cohort. Basic Education in the Arts might also be considered elitist because parents have to pay relatively high student fees. However, there are currently negotiations and efforts to create more inclusive measures that will grant access to children from all social backgrounds.[59] Jaana Räsänen and Pihla Meskanen also drew attention to reports by founders of a new school of architecture for children and young people in Tampere, which illustrate that it is also not easy for start-ups to be included in the Basic Education in the Arts program.

In spring 2018, the Tiili School of Architecture was founded as a charitable institution by a team of six and chaired by Ruud Ronni. Its point of departure was the School Club Program, which Archinfo Finland launched under Jaana Räsänen in 2016 in order to strengthen the national network for architecture education in places where Basic Education in the Arts programs or other courses were not yet available.[60] By autumn 2018, clubs had been set up at three schools as part of the two-year program. According to board member and Tiili school teacher Else Luotinen, the school clubs offer weekly 90-minute work sessions with children aged 6 to 19.[61] The program has been supported by the Ministry of Education and Culture, but also by SAFA and other organizations and sponsors, such as local architecture firms. That way, the teachers' fees are paid, and Ruud Ronni was able, as he explained, to be employed as a local contact person for SAFA and use his working time to set up the school. All other work is done on a voluntary basis.[62] The school could currently not be included in the Basic Education in the Arts program as it did not have enough stability to guarantee a headmaster and permanent teachers. In order to be able to teach within the framework of Basic Education in the Arts, continuity as well as specific course content must be guaranteed. This will not be possible for the school in the near future until they receive more extensive funding to cover fees, marketing, rent, materials, and administrative and insurance costs.[63] They had applied for a comprehensive grant, but it was not awarded because the Tiili School did not yet have the necessary references.

Pihla Meskanen also reported on the long process of obtaining state funding for ARKKI. From 2003 onwards, funding under the Basic Education in the Arts Act would have been possible. Although the curriculum had long been completed and approved, ARKKI did not receive funding until 2008. "The system of funding works so that, once you get it, it is continuous. This is what makes it difficult for new institutions and schools, as the total funding budget needs to get bigger before new schools can receive funding."[64] According to Jaana Räsänen, the system is currently being opened up, so that it will also be possible to apply for subsidies for new start-ups, but this process will also require some stamina.[65] This may explain why, so far, there have been so few architecture schools for children and young people and why the Tiili School was opened 25 years after the founding of ARKKI and Lastu. Currently, the school is still small. According to Else Luotinen, there were a total of 17 students in the first school year of 2019, with five of the participants from the first semester having registered for the follow-up course in autumn. Luotinen estimates that a total of about 130 to 200 students have participated in courses or school clubs since autumn 2018, although they cannot offer school clubs in the current autumn semester due to a lack of teachers. However, courses at two to five schools are planned again for spring 2020, depending on the number of teachers available.[66]

Conclusion: Integrate Baukultur into the educational system!

One of the most surprising findings that the examination of the Finnish educational system has brought to light is that—contrary to what is generally assumed in Germany—the Finnish school system no longer has a particularly high proportion of arts education, and architecture education is far less present in the *National Core Curricula* than might be expected. On both points, there is even the impression that Germany could be much better positioned, at least formally. For example, in Germany, art education is a compulsory course for the first ten grades, and pupils now in theory have a high chance of being taught by trained arteducators from the first to the last grade, since these types of educator are increasingly more accepted in the primary school sector and academic qualifications in this area are supported accordingly. As an example, the framework curriculum for Berlin shows that Baukultur education—or rather the focus on "architecture and space"—is provided for all grades through the subject of art.[67]

While Finnish architecture education seems to have a higher presence in actual school life than the curricula would suggest—which is due to the specific historical situation but is also the result of a consistent architectural policy that has now been in place for more than 20 years—, the situation in Germany is the exact opposite. It seems almost surprising that Baukultur education is present in the framework curricula as it is still hardly considered in actual school life. A study on the situation of architecture education in German schools is still pending, hence it is difficult to make reliable statements about the quality and quantity of architecture education. It can be assumed, however, that the situation will be approximately comparable to that of Swiss schools. Here, as a recent study has shown, pupils only sporadically come into contact with topics relating to architecture education.[68] So far, architecture education has not really found its way into teacher training in Germany. It currently depends on the personal interest of individual teachers whether pupils come into contact with architecture or Baukultur during their regular schooling. Only the Bauhaus-Universität Weimar maintained an exemplary long-term cooperation between the architecture degree and the art teacher training.[69] However, this has remained an isolated case and currently seems to exist only rudimentarily in the form of a lecture series.

The *National Curriculum for Basic Education in the Arts* also shows that architecture education in Finland is much broader in content than what is currently understood under the German keyword "Baukulturelle Bildung" (Baukultur education). In Finland, architecture education is actually designed as civic education and is aimed at bringing general knowledge of Baukultur to the public—knowledge which is necessary for taking responsibility in planning processes that affect one's own environment or ensuring the protection of built heritage, as laid down in the Land Use and Building Act, but also in the basic rights catalog of the constitution. In contrast, Baukultur education in Germany is still largely equated with crafting, building, and construction—which is also largely reflected in the proposals in *Bildungsorte und*

Lernwelten der Baukultur (Educational Venues and Learning Worlds of Baukultur), a study published by the Wüstenrot Stiftung in 2019.[70] This approach is undoubtedly justified, as crafting and building are among the central aesthetic practices by which children acquire and explore the world. However, it would be welcome if the projects were more closely linked to Baukultur content and learning objectives, and, as in Finland, focused more on promoting an overall understanding of built environments and architecture. Moreover, it is noticeable that the child's perspective is far too rarely taken into account in German projects and concepts. Yet children already bring extensive knowledge of architecture and built environments with them and are specialists in both subjects in their living environments and at school. It is to be welcomed, however, that the potential of actual urban spaces as learning venues has also been discovered and is increasingly included in German school projects.[71]

Just how different the fundamental attitudes in Finland and Germany are can also be seen in the self-image of the Federal Chamber of German Architects, which—with their "Architecture in Schools" program—are the main actors tasked with carrying out teaching projects in schools. Their focus, however, is on the "building contractor of tomorrow," as can be seen from its program text: The Federal State Chambers of Architects want everyone to develop an understanding of the built environment and thus become qualified building owners and competent decision-makers in politics, administration, and business."[72] Their counterpart, the Finnish Association of Architects SAFA, further defined the objectives of civic education in architecture in its 2001 report *Discovering Architecture*, which took into account those citizens who ultimately have to live with the decisions of architects, planners, and politicians: "The built environment," it states, "provides a framework for all of us to act and to fulfill ourselves. It constitutes the greatest part of our national wealth and belongs to all of us, the builders and the users. All citizens should therefore have an active understanding of the built environment, regardless of age, profession or educational background."[73]

1 Cf. Korpelainen and Yanar 2001, p.6.
2 Cf. Korpelainen and Yanar 2001, p.6.
3 Tiina Valpola via email, December 19, 2019.
4 Cf. Korpelainen and Yanar 2001, pp.18–19.
5 Cf. Meskanen 2012, 2; cf. Kataikko 2006.
6 Cf. Perusopetuksen opetussuunnitelman perusteet 2004 (NCC for Basic Education 2004). https://www.oph.fi/sites/default/files/documents/perusopetuksen-opetussuunnitelman-perusteet_2004.pdf, p.237 (accessed December 28, 2019).
7 Cf. Religion grade 1-2, pp.143–148; grade 3-6, pp.264–271; and cf. the chapter on religion in the NCC for General Upper Secondary Schools 2016, p.277.
8 Cf. NCC for Basic Education 2016, p.157.
9 Cf. NCC for Basic Education 2016, p.275.
10 Cf. NCC for Basic Education 2016, p.415; cf. NCC for General Upper Secondary Schools 2016, p.201.
11 Cf. NCC for Basic Education 2016, pp.139–143.
12 Cf. NCC for Basic Education 2016, p.139; p.256.
13 Cf. NCC for General Upper Secondary Schools 2016, p.277.
14 Cf. NCC for General Upper Secondary Schools 2016, p.202, pp.241–56, p.266.
15 Mikko Hartikainen in conversation with the author, May 7, 2019.
16 Cf. NCC for Basic Education 2016, pp.153–55, pp.286–88, pp.458–60.
17 Cf. NCC for Basic Education 2016, p.153, p.286, p.458 and cf. NCC for General Upper Secondary Schools 2016, p.275.
18 Cf. Aiming for transversal competence, T7, NCC for Basic Education 2016, pp.21–26.
19 NCC for Basic Education 2016, p.25.
20 Cf. NCC for Basic Education 2016, pp.30–31.
21 Mikko Hartikainen in conversation with the author, May 7, 2019.
22 Cf. https://www.lastenkulttuuri.fi/en/cultural-education-plan/ (accessed December 28, 2019).
23 Mikko Hartikainen in conversation with the author, May 7, 2019; cf. NCC for Basic Education 2016, p.99.
24 Cf. https://www.slideshare.net/jukkasormunen/presentation-of-educational-structure-in-kuopio-and-finland-education-system-242019, p.26 (accessed December 28, 2019).
25 Cf. Architectural Policy Program of Kuopio, 2007, p.21, and Second Architectural Policy Program of Koupio, 2017.
26 Cf. https://www.kuopio.fi/documents/7369547/7450879/Apoli_250x210_FINAL_web.pdf/00136840-82ff-493f-a8e4-c559a522bc0d, p.36, measure 27 (accessed December 28, 2019).
27 Mervi Eskelinen in Skype conversation, June 6, 2019.
28 NCC for Basic Education 2016, p.33.
29 Pihla Meskanen in conversation with the author, May 9, 2019.
30 Cf. Jaana Räsänen's guest article in this publication.
31 Cf. NCC for Basic Education 2016, p.31.
32 Cf. Räsänen's guest article in this publication.
33 Riikka Mäkikoskela in conversation with the author, May 13, 2019.
34 Henna Haavisto in conversation with the author, May 10, 2019.
35 Lotta Leskelä in phone conversation, August 30, 2019.
36 Mikko Hartikainen in conversation with the author, May 7, 2019; cf. Pohjakallio-Koskinen 2010.
37 Riikka Mäkikoskela in conversation with the author, May 13, 2019.
38 Henna Haavisto in conversation with the author, May 10, 2019; Riikka Mäkikoskela in conversation with the author, May 13, 2019.

39 Martti Raevaara in Skype conversation, June 6, 2019.
40 Cf. https://minedu.fi/en/basic-education-in-arts (accessed December 28, 2019).
41 Cf. Hartikainen (2009), p. 7.
42 Cf. Heinimaa 2007.
43 Cf. Heinimaa 2007.
44 Cf. Hartikainen (2009), p. 7–8.
45 Cf. NCC Basic Education in the Arts 2018, p. 23.
46 Cf. NCC Basic Education in the Arts 2018, p. 23.
47 Cf. NCC Basic Education in the Arts 2018, p. 24.
48 Cf. NCC Basic Education in the Arts 2018, p. 18, p. 86.
49 Cf. NCC Basic Education in the Arts 2018, p. 26.
50 Cf. NCC Basic Education in the Arts 2018, p. 95.
51 Cf. NCC Basic Education in the Arts 2018, p. 26, p. 95.
52 Klaus Savolainen via email June 6, 2019.
53 Ilpo Vuorela via email, June 15, 2019.
54 Riikka Mäkikoskela in conversation with the author, May 13, 2019.
55 Cf. Kanerva and Mitchell 2017, p. 96.
56 Cf. Hietala 2017, p. 6.
57 Mikko Hartikainen in conversation with the author, May 7, 2019.
58 Cf. Hietala (2017), p. 9.
59 Riikka Mäkikoskela in conversation with the author, May 13, 2019.
60 Cf. http://archinfo.fi/2019/11/arkkitehtuurikerhot-2016-2019-hanke-nosti-arkkitehtuurikasvatuksen-saavutettavuutta-valtakunnallisesti/ (accessed January 1, 2020).
61 Else Luotinen via email, December 3, 2019.
62 Ruud Ronni via email, December 3, 2019.
63 Else Luotinen via email, December 3, 2019. The legal requirements for teaching within the framework of Basic Education in the Arts are laid down in the Basic Education in the Arts Act 1998/633 §3.
64 Pihla Meskanen in conversation with the author, May 9, 2019.
65 Jaana Räsänen in conversation with the author, May 9, 2019.
66 Else Luotinen via email, December 3, 2019.
67 Cf. https://www.berlin.de/sen/bildung/unterricht/faecher-rahmen-lehrplaene/rahmenlehrplaene/ (accessed January 7, 2020).
68 Cf. Archijeunes (2019), p. 26.
69 Cf. Hubrich 2006a + b
70 Cf. Wüstenrot Stiftung 2019, pp. 30–81.
71 Examples include the "Stadtentdecker" projects of the Brandenburg Chamber of Architects (2013), the "Stadtspäher" project, which the Technical University of Dortmund carried out in 2013/14 in cooperation with the Wüstenrot Stiftung, or the "Stadtteildetektive" project of the German Museum of Architecture in Frankfurt, which has been running for several years.
72 https://www.bak.de/baukultur/architektur-macht-schule/ (accessed January 7, 2020).
73 Korpelainen and Yanar 2001, p. 4

Institutions in architecture education

Architecture education at university level

Architecture education is less well established at Finnish universities, with regard to teacher training, than one would expect given the prominent role that architecture plays in the educational system.[1] Several of the interviewed actors confirmed that a great need still exists in this area and expressed the same opinion as Pihla Meskanen, who stated that "universities used to be closed units, which decided independently on their fields of interest. We only have three universities for architecture and maybe three or four for teacher training. Now with Aalto University, students have a vast possibility to study cross-disciplinary studies from various faculties."[2] On the one hand, it is evident that architectural history, as already described in chapter 4, plays a significant role in the training of art teachers and that students can take classes in the field of built environment education. On the other hand, a systematic integration of architecture education into teacher training, as called for in the 1998 *Architectural Policy*, does not yet seem to be in place. Since it has not been possible to establish direct contact with either the University of Helsinki or the University of Lapland in Rovaniemi, the following remarks are based primarily on observations made by Prof. Martti Raevaara, head of the Master's program in art education and head of the Department of Art at Aalto University.

According to Raevaara, architecture education is primarily present in an indirect way at the two universities where art teachers are trained, namely the University of Lapland in Rovaniemi and Aalto University in Espoo. While the University of Lapland focuses more on the Arctic culture and environment, especially with regard to the Arctic habitat, the research at Aalto University centers more on the city and urban life. According to Raevaara, art education in Finland has since the 1960s and 1970s focused on environmental education, particularly highlighting architecture, planning, and participation. "When I was a student in the late 1970s—I graduated in 1981—, we had a number of electives in which we visited suburbs together with architects and urban planning offices. It was all about perception; it was about understanding the power structures in the background. It was the post-war era. People moved to the cities and apartments were in high demand. It was a very hectic time in architecture. Back then, the training that art teachers received focused on the environment and social aspects."[3] Raevaara pointed out that he was not speaking about environmental education within the primary school sector, which is a subject in its own right, but that he was concerned with a component of art education at large. Art education was, however, not greatly concerned with architecture but instead focused on a combination of civic education and an understanding of environmental issues.[4] Yet this changed during the 1980s and 1990s. More electives were added, and in the 1990s and 2000s, digitalization became a more important issue, and modelling became part of art teacher training.

Raevaara expressed regret that much of what happened in art education in the 1960s and 1970s no longer occurs today. "We are now so strongly focused on sustainability issues that understanding of power structures and decision making in urban planning is too little emphasized. Today, we also use a lot of content for visualizations, for 3D modeling—virtual reality is now strongly on the rise, and artificial intelligence is also an important part of our studies."[5] While in the 1980s and 1990s art teacher training was, according to Raevaara, still strongly geared towards art and design, it is today much more openly oriented towards multi- and trans-disciplinary cooperation. This can also be seen as a result of the creation of Aalto University by a merger of three universities in 2010, the University of Art and Design Helsinki, the Helsinki University of Technology, and the Helsinki School of Economics.

Due to this new orientation, recent years have shown that the scope of activities of art teachers has also expanded considerably. According to Raevaara, educators no longer automatically work as teachers in schools, but are also actors in museums, municipalities, and libraries, or become entrepreneurs.[6]

Since the teaching profession is highly regarded in Finland and many young people want to study art, as Raevaara explains, Aalto University has found itself in the enviable position of being able to select the best 15 students for its Bachelor's degree from a pool of 250 to 300 applicants each year, and the same number of students from 60 to 70 applicants for its Master's program. The university focuses particularly on the Master's program, which addresses so-called professionals—candidates who have already earned an academic degree, preferably in an artistic field—and offers them the chance to receive a pedagogical education and subject studies in art education in order to become certified art teachers. Because all Bachelor's students will continue to Master's studies too, together with the vocational Master's program students, there are a total of around 200 students in the field of art education at Aalto University.

Unlike comparable programs at German universities, this Master's program was not established in order to facilitate a lateral entry and thus compensate for an acute lack of teaching staff, but it was set up rather to be able to respond adequately to innovations and trends in the art world and therefore remain closely tied to artistic practices.[7] Raevaara reported, for instance, that two landscape architects are currently students in the Master's program: "Of course, they no longer have to take art classes, since they are already well trained in this background. They instead focus on art education and pedagogical studies." Usually, students have to earn 120 credits, which is the scope of the Master's degree. However, all students in the vocational Master's program have a personal study plan based on their former education and work experience. Special topics such as architecture education are integrated into the department through this Master's program, as the "professionals" are individually supported in developing a didactic approach for their respective discipline, which they can later apply in their professional lives and implement into the peer group learning processes that are part of their studies. In this way, architecture education finds its way into the training of art teachers.[8]

Contrary to what might be expected given Finland's pioneering position in the field of architecture education, however, this has not been systematically anchored at the university level. Explicit research posts or professorships, in which independent didactics for architecture education could be worked out and teaching materials or textbooks could be developed based on practical research, are not yet available in Finland either. As early as 2001, the report *Discovering Architecture* pointed out that although civic education in architecture is active and widespread in Finland, its future depends on how it develops. "Very little research has been carried out in this field. A broader and deeper knowledge of both content and didactics requires research, which can be purely theoretical, but must remain closely related to the practical aspects of teaching."[9]

Even today, architecture mediators in Finland are not yet specifically trained but still have to find their own individual way, even if, as the Master's program offered at Aalto University shows, they receive more support today than did the preceding generation of mediators. Many mediators such as Pihla Meskanen, Jaana Räsänen, Ilpo Vuorela, or Ruud Ronni initially trained as architects and then added a pedagogical degree to their profile while others, such as Mervi Eskelinen or Lotta Leskelä, are trained art teachers who then advanced into the field of architecture. Today, it is somewhat easier than it was in the 1990s to engage in interdisciplinary studies thanks to the bachelor-master system, a tendency that is further facilitated by the fusion of Helsinki's three universities. Jaana Räsänen speaks about how her career unfolded: "When I studied architecture at the University of Oulu, I was also interested in education and attended some classes there. I received my first degree in 'Basics of Education' in the Department of Behavioral Science and 'Environmental Education' in the Department of Teacher Education and combined it with my degree in architecture. Since the former universities of technology (architecture and engineering), art and design (including art education), and economic sciences in Helsinki have been merged into Aalto University, it has become easier to combine these two subjects. Yet the students still need to take initiative and organize themselves."[10] Pihla Meskanen recommends that architects who want to become architecture mediators take basic education seminars or independent online courses on pedagogy.[11] For a while, the only possibility to receive the specific and officially advanced education that would allow you to become a certified architecture educator was a summer university program at the University of Kuopio. During a 15-month advanced education program, which ran from September 19, 2014, to December 31, 2015, a group of 20 participants, half of whom were art teachers and the other half art educators from the curatorial field,[12] were officially trained as certified architecture educators. This 20-credit "Messenger of Architecture" program was organized by the Hannes Snellman Summer University in cooperation with Archinfo Finland, the Lastu School and other individuals active in the field of architecture education, as Lotta Leskelä, curator of the education department at the Alvar Aalto Museum in Jyväskylä, explained.[13]

Conversations with Pihla Meskanen and Jaana Räsänen from the ARKKI School of Architecture and Mervi Eskelinen from the Lastu School made it clear that architecture and visual arts schools often cannot fall back on trained architecture mediators but usually have to train and educate their own teachers. However, the fact not only that architecture schools have to train their own staff, but that this generally applies to all visual arts schools, became clear when talking to Riikka Mäkikoskela, director of the Finnish Association of Art Schools for Children and Young People. She pointed out that even certified art teachers have to be trained, as they do not yet have the necessary preparation to work with younger children. According to the general school system, school children up to the 6th grade are taught by their class teachers and not by trained art educators. The Finnish Association of Art Schools for Children and Young People, for instance, provides artists with pedagogical methods and at the same time trains art teachers in how to apply artistic methods and didactics for younger children. "We 'complete' the pedagogical skillset of both artists and art teachers to enable them to teach in the participating schools. Because we do so, we are financially supported by the Finnish National Agency for Education: this confirms that private art schools in Finland are particularly important for younger children, who are usually taught by class teachers from grade 1 to 6 and not by trained art teachers."[14]

ARKKI, Lastu, and others

One of the most interesting findings from the conversations with Finnish individuals involved in the field of architecture education is that specialized know-how is not primarily to be found at the universities, but rather lies in the hands of private institutions and their members. Occasionally, this know-how is transferred to universities, for instance through temporary teaching assignments or programs like the Summer Academy in Kuopio.

The two architecture schools for children and young people, ARKKI and Lastu, both of which have been active since 1993, are among the most important institutions promoting architecture education in Finland. Even though the number of students engaged in the Basic Education in the Arts curriculum is relatively low, the importance of private schools of architecture for children and young people in Finland is immense and their influence enormous, as both schools offer a wide range of courses, workshops, project weeks, holiday camps, and teacher training, as well as cooperating with schools in addition to providing an ongoing long-term program. A total of 40 teachers—seven of whom are full-time employees—work for ARKKI, whose headquarters are located in an old cable factory in Helsinki. Here 600 students are hosted every week. ARKKI also has small branches in the neighboring cities of Vantaa and Espoo, where another 70 and 75 children are taught respectively. In addition, the architecture school cooperates with museums, schools, and cities. In the much smaller Lastu School in Lapinlahti, a rural community in central Finland with only 9,000 inhabitants, the commitment goes far beyond Basic Education in the Arts, which only plays a minor part with 50 school children involved and, due to the small number of students, merely offers the *general syllabus* of Basic Education in the Arts. Yet the school, which was founded by Mervi Eskelinen in 1993, and its staff consisting of 10 employees, offers a multi-faceted program in addition to Basic Education in the Arts. Unlike at ARKKI, where working with adults is limited to parent-child courses in the pre-school sector, this also includes an extensive program within the framework of adult education. According to Eskelinen, these classes are attended by experts such as craftspeople or educators, but also by laypeople interested in civic education. Eskelinen further explained that there are plans to expand the range of classes for adults in the direction of Basic Education in the Arts, as there have definitely been requests for this. These requests have, for instance, been made by teachers who would like to work with children in this field—in such cases an extensive advanced training program would make sense. Yet parents and other personally invested people have also shown great interest in the program.[15]

As early as 2001, the two schools of architecture, ARKKI and Lastu, were presented as lighthouse projects of Finnish architecture education, for instance in SAFA's report *Discovering Architecture,* which certainly also contributed to the fact that a somewhat distorted impression had been created regarding the scope and availability of architecture education in Finland. Yet the importance of ARKKI in particular, which now runs international franchises because its curricula have been copied so often,[16] cannot be overestimated for the development of architecture education. Why it took 25 years for Tiili, the first new school of architecture for children, to be founded can be gleaned from the descriptions by Else Luotinen and Ruud Ronni, which show that it is—even in Finland—by no means easy to found an architecture school, to obtain appropriate subsidies and a license for the Basic Education in the Arts program. What is more, Luotinen's observations also show that even in Finland, in a university city like Tampere with a population of 228,000, the success of an architecture school for children and young people cannot be taken for granted. Instead, demand for this must first be slowly built up, even if, as in the case of Tiili, its curriculum has already been effectively introduced through the provision of school clubs offered in several schools in the city.

Yet the fact that 25 years passed before a new attempt was made to set up an architecture school for children and young people, as well as the observation that Finnish architecture education is clearly rooted in the early 1990s, also allude to other specific circumstances, which were mentioned in several expert talks: the massive economic crisis that shook Finland for years in the early 1990s. With the entire construction sector in a state of collapse, many architecture graduates decided to continue their studies at university for longer and chose to pursue a degree in education or art education. This trend was also influenced by the fact that they suddenly seemed to have time to think about more fundamental things and consider what could be improved, adapted, or changed. In this way, a breeding ground and the right climate for the development of the *Architectural Policy* and new concepts for architecture education were created.[17] This was ultimately also favored by the Basic Education in the Arts Act, which passed in 1992 and for the first time put architecture on an equal footing with the other arts and made it possible to teach architecture as a component of arts programs. ARKKI and Lastu were established in 1993, while the architecture department at the Visual Arts School in Jyväskylä was developed in 1996, a year after the Erkkeri School in Turku had been founded. No information on the fate of the Erkkeri School in Turku could be obtained for this study, except for Jaana Räsänen's statement that the local Arts Council made an unsuccessful attempt to revive it when developing a local architectural policy for Turku in 2009.[18]

After the adoption of the *Architectural Policy* in 1998 and until the establishment of Archinfo Finland in 2013, the architectural institutions that also played a major role in the development of the *Architectural Policy* in 1998, namely the Museum of Finnish Architecture in Helsinki, the Alvar Aalto Museum in Jyväskylä, and, in particular, the Finnish Association of Architects SAFA, became significant players in the promotion of architecture education. As early as 1980, SAFA published a document that is now viewed as a pioneering step, a comprehensive kit for environmental education, *Viihtyisä ympäristö* (Agreeable Environment), which consisted of a handbook for teachers, tasks, and overhead transparencies. It also came with a set of slides depicting the history of

Finland's built environment, posters showing a typical village development, and an activity book for schoolchildren.[19] SAFA was, as has already been described, instrumental in communicating and implementing the *Architectural Policy* until the position of special advisor for architecture for the National Council for Architecture was established in the Ministry for Education in 2004, and was also particularly responsible for the development of architecture education until the establishment of Archinfo Finland. In 2001, SAFA, in cooperation with the Arts Council of Finland (now Arts Promotion Centre), published the report *Discovering Architecture. Civic Education in Architecture in Finland*, which for the first time presented a comprehensive overview of schools, initiatives, and teaching methods but also of teaching materials and advanced education and support opportunities.[20] In the following years, SAFA was also instrumental in developing school and teaching materials. In 2004 and 2007, SAFA cooperated with Jaana Räsänen, who then held the post of architectural advisor for the Helsinki-Uusima region, to publish two textbooks: *Arkkitehtuurin ABC. Löytöretki rakennettuun ympäristöön* (The ABC of Architecture 1. A voyage of discovery into the built environment) and *Arkkitehtuurin ABC 2: Peruskäsitteitä* (The ABC of Architecture 2. Basic concepts).[21] These two books set out guidelines for architecture lessons in community schools and high-school education, which were supplemented by Anna Hänninen's publication *Matkalla arkkitehtuurin maahan* (On a Journey to Architecture) in 2007, which is addressed to art teachers in kindergartens and primary schools.[22]

One of the most interesting projects initiated through the cooperation of various institutions, including SAFA, the Museum of Finnish Architecture, the Design Museum Helsinki, and the Uusima Arts Council, was the "Ampiainen" theme day on architecture and design, which was held in schools throughout Finland for the first time in 2005.[23] "The idea of the project was to bring architecture and design education to schools. We arranged workshops, teacher training, visits by experts in architecture and design, and published an annual magazine to share experiences and ideas. In the end, there was a design competition and an exhibition of the best student works," as Jaana Räsänen described the initiative, which was carried out until 2010 and discontinued after she ended her term as regional artist for architecture education in the Uusima Arts Council.[24]

The Alvar Aalto Foundation in Jyväskylä also made an important contribution to the development and promotion of architecture education with the international workshop series "Soundings for Architecture," which was dedicated to the topic of architecture education in 2003, 2004, and 2006 (Soundings 4-6).[25] After lengthy discussions, which were already initiated at the 4th Soundings Conference in 2003, the international network "Playce" for the promotion of architecture education was, as Teija Isohauta points out, founded at the 5th conference in August 2004. The name "Playce" is a combination of the terms "play" and "space."[26] In 2006 the network already had members from 16 European nations as well as the USA and Japan, says Päivi Kataikko.[27] In the early years, "Playce" was very active, as Pihla Meskanen reported: "The members invited each other to meetings once or twice a year and organized joint workshops, but this exchange has in the past few years no longer worked in the same way, simply because a lot of activities started in all countries and everyone has a lot on their hands."[28] The "Playce" meetings have since been replaced by the series of international conferences "Creating the Future I-III," organized by ARKKI, which have been held every five years in 2009, 2014, and 2019.[29]

Recent trends in architecture education in Finland

The methods and strategies currently used in Finland to mediate architecture can also be studied using the example of the country's two most important architecture museums, the Museum of Finnish Architecture in Helsinki and the Alvar Aalto Museum in Jyväskylä. Both institutions offer an extensive educational program for children and young people and train multipliers and teachers respectively. Since 2019, the Museum of Finnish Architecture has featured a newly designed, freely accessible educational space, the so-called A&O Room, in which various activities and workshops take place, such as a regularly offered toddler class for parents with small children or the traditional gingerbread workshop in December, in which 300 children build a gingerbread model city in the style of the 1960s, which is then exhibited in the museum's foyer.[30] In addition, according to the museum's Head of Collaboration and Engagement, Arja-Liisa Kaasinen, it offers workshops for pupils of all ages and free information material is made available for teachers who can download and use it specifically for lessons at different grades. Kaasinen explains that this offer also includes an online game in which children and young people can test their stylistic knowledge of modern architecture and compete against one another.[31] In addition to this activity program, which is something one would perhaps expect in this context, there are two exceptionally remarkable concepts among the teaching materials that can be downloaded from the museum's website: these provisions show that the Museum of Finnish Architecture in no way shies away from contemporary or everyday architecture and that it understands its task of introducing people to architecture as going far beyond its traditional museum collections. These are practical mediation strategies that are intended to contribute to a fundamental sensitization toward architecture. As a starting point, the website offers a toolkit that can be downloaded, with the help of which students of all grades can explore their school building. "Maailman paras koulutehtäväsarja" (The World's Best School Task Set) has been developed in cooperation with ARKKI and includes concrete instructions that students of all grades can follow in order to, first of all, explore and document their school building from a variety of perspectives. In a second step, they are encouraged to use these observations to develop their own visions, which are collected and ultimately brought together in a participatory school of the future. After the research phase, all students design their ideal dream classroom using a wide variety of materials, but with one standardized size. In the final step, these dream classrooms are fitted together in a participatory negotiation process and finally become an ideal school building.[32]

That the Museum of Finnish Architecture is interested in encouraging students to generally discuss and explore architecture, and to acknowledge that everyone is an expert in their own built environment,[33] is also demonstrated by the concept "Ten Keys to Architecture," which is available for download from the website. This remarkably simple yet highly effective little online publication promises: "These questions will help you to explore every building!"[34] This statement is followed by ten short, significant observation assignments on the themes of form, space, movement, material, structure, color, light, sound, detail, and atmosphere, which show how refreshingly simple and unpretentious architecture education can be. For example, under the heading of movement, it says: "What are main and which ones are minor rooms? How are the rooms that serve the house's different purposes arranged? Who is in the rooms? How does the room influence the way people move in it? Can you discover unused rooms or areas?"[35] In relation to structure, the following questions are raised: "Can you identify structures that carry loads? Can you sense compression or pulling? ... Gravity is not visible, but what other weights could the building support?"[36] The museum does not impart specialist knowledge here, but rather provides practical, low-threshold suggestions that show that anyone can view and explore architecture and that no professional expertise is necessary.

The Alvar Aalto Museum in Jyväskylä also surprises with fresh, forward-looking mediation strategies. Lotta Leskelä, curator of the education department, reported in an interview that her main task in the museum is first and foremost classic mediation. She plans and leads workshops and guided tours of the exhibitions and designs programs for temporary exhibitions. In addition, she develops workshops for the broader public, yet a large part of her work involves working with school classes: "The cultural education plan of the city of Jyväskylä intends that each student visiting the local public school visits a cultural institution once a year. For example, first-graders go to the Natural History Museum, second-graders go to the Craft Museum, and 9-to 10-year-olds go to the Alvar Aalto Museum—in total, about 1,500 children visit us every year. In the course of the two-hour program, they first get a one-hour guided tour of the permanent exhibition and then spend another hour in the museum's workshop room, where an urban planning project is currently under way."[37]

The fact that the Alvar Aalto Foundation, which according to Jaana Räsänen is one of the pioneers of architecture education in Finland alongside the two architecture schools for children,[38] ARKKI and Lastu, as well as the Jyväskylä Art School, still lives up to its reputation today is shown by the concept of Alvar Aalto Schools, which Leskelä drew attention to. The network of Alvar Aalto Cities was established in 2017 with the aim of increasing public awareness of the renowned architect's works in cities with Aalto-designed architecture both in Finland and abroad. It is coordinated by the Alvar Aalto Foundation and seeks to create a space to exchange mutual ideas, as a result of which the foundation established the network of Alvar Aalto Schools in April 2019.[39] This decision was made with the aim of creating a network of schools, initially only involving the Finnish Alvar Aalto Cities, that promotes architecture education. "The idea emerged before the background," says Lotta Leskelä, "that we believe that architecture is a phenomenon that is well suited for cross-curricular teaching and could provide a good basis for many school projects. We are trying to develop a network in the frame of which schools can cooperate with each other and develop materials together." It is, as Leskelä describes, a voluntary program embracing 14 schools as members at the time of the interview. At the founding meeting in April 2019, common topics were discussed and, for the year 2019/2020, the theme "Aalto in everyday life" was chosen. The participating schools have already begun to work with this first theme. "We want the teachers to work on these topics both independently and together to exchange ideas and motivate each other. It is about communicating that architecture education is simple. You can observe your home, your environment, your classroom. You can draw or measure the classroom. Many teachers think that it is difficult to communicate architecture. We would like to take away that fear and want to show them that it is easy to bring architecture into schools and that it is important because we live in buildings and urban environments. It is important that we understand that we can influence our environment."[40] In its basic structure, the concept is similar to the two mediation strategies presented by the Museum of Finnish Architecture, which also show that it is easy to mediate architecture, and that no museum or special architecture is needed for this, but that it can also be applied to ubiquitous everyday architecture.

"If possible," Leskelä added, "we would like to create teaching materials, but we do not yet know how to accomplish that. We have only had one meeting so far and need to develop our activities first. However, many teachers were interested in the network." According to Leskelä, only one or two network meetings are planned to take place each year—in between she can visit schools and give advice on request—but the main aim is to establish a network that is ultimately self-sustaining. To support this endeavor, she will start a Facebook group and send out regular newsletters. "The network can start out small at the beginning, but we can develop it further and see what the teachers want and what will become important in the future." As a possible example, Leskelä, who encourages pupils and teachers to be "experiencer," mentioned a project that the Alvar Aalto Foundation carried out at the time of the interview with a school in Säynätsalo, a district of Jyväskylä that gained international fame through its town hall building, which was designed by Alvar Aalto. The project "MunTour" invited children to develop their own guided tours of the area and to record their observations, stories, and ideas in a script, which they could then use to guide parents, friends, and other guests. According to Leskelä, such a project could easily be incorporated into the network of Alvar Aalto Schools. A template guide could also be produced so that other

Fig. 19

schools could adopt the concept. After all, they all have at least one building designed by Alvar Aalto in their city.[41]

It is remarkable that a number of similar projects have emerged throughout Finland in recent years, in which resources have been wisely pooled and many multipliers could be reached at very little cost in time and resources. Most of these projects were either initiated by Archinfo Finland or carried out in cooperation with this body. One of the most successful and effective projects initiated by Archinfo Finland under Jaana Räsänen is the School Club Program, which has been running since 2016 in cooperation with seven Finnish cities—Seinäjoki, Tampere, Turku, Oulu, Uusikaupunki, Helsinki, and Jyväskylä—and which has already been mentioned in connection with the newly founded Tiili School of Architecture in Tampere.[42] The program seeks to expand national provisions in the field of architecture education and to give even more children throughout Finland the chance to turn architecture into a hobby. To this end, a 90-minute after-school workshop is offered once a week in partner schools, so that around 130 children are introduced to architecture every year.

The "Salvos" project, which the Finnish Association of Art Schools for Children and Young People ran from 2016 to 2018 in cooperation with Archinfo Finland, was also highly effective and wide-ranging. The project addressed arts schools wishing to strengthen architecture education as part of their visual arts programs within the framework of Basic Education in the Arts. It was developed against the background of the new curriculum for the Basic Education in the Arts program, which came into force in 2018 and defined new target areas for the visual arts, such as visual literacy, its relationship to other arts, inclusion, and the exertion of influence. Four arts schools from Valkeakoski,

Lohja, Lappeenranta, and Lahti cooperated in the project, which focused on teacher training as well as peer learning. The aim was to improve and strengthen the knowledge and awareness of teachers and students in relation to architectural and environmental education through a number of pilot projects. The 38 projects presented in the Salvos brochure demonstrate that the schools' immediate vicinity was always used as a learning environment and that children and young people were invited to participate in planning processes and create their own artworks in public space. With experimental collaborative teaching methods developed within the project, the approximately 1,000 children and young people participating at the four schools were taught to enhance their ability to consciously observe but also to form a personal relationship with their built and natural environment.[43]

Many Archinfo Finland projects, such as "Meidän paikka 2018" (My Place) or "Eilen, tänään, huomenna 2013-14" (Yesterday, Today, Tomorrow), to name just a couple, were designed as teacher training courses but carried out in tandem with educational activities involving children and young people. The "Meidän paikka" project, funded by the Finnish National Agency of Education, is about providing guidance to 7th to 9th grade students who explore their learning environment and unite to revive a neglected or forgotten place, thereby learning to participate, collaborate, and exert their influence. In the project "Eilen, tänään, huomenna," children from 8 to 9 years of age explored their city center, developed ideas, tested out different interactions and work methods, and produced teaching materials that engaged with the topic of participation.[44] It is remarkable that at the end of each project, toolkits were created which are now available for other teachers to use and develop further.[45]

These toolkits, which also include the two concepts designed by the Museum of Finnish Architecture, represent a novel form of teaching material that appears to replace the classic textbook. After the urgent need for teaching materials was formulated in the 2001 report *Discovering Architecture*, classic textbooks were brought out, such as *Matkalla arkkitehtuurin maahan. Lasten arkkitehtuurikasvatuksen työ- ja opaskirja opettajille* (On the Journey to Architecture. Workbook and Guide to Architecture Education of Children for Teachers) by Anna Hänninen from 2007, which focuses on kindergarten children and younger schoolchildren, or the previously mentioned ABC publications designed for secondary levels I and II, which Jaana Räsänen developed in cooperation with SAFA.[46] The trend towards the toolkit, which formulates clearly defined tasks with precise details of the target group and teaching content that can be applied in school lessons, began with the *Architecture Toolkit,* which the Nordic Playce Group developed in 2009. This *Architecture Toolkit* is now available in nine languages and consists of a colorful, house-shaped cardboard box containing 13 large-format, sturdy task cards and four sensory tools—a hand mirror, a funnel, an eye mask, and fingerless gloves—these are supposed to help children explore architecture and the built environment using all their senses.[47] In 2013, the toolkit *Tilat, talot & kaupungit* (Rooms, Houses & Cities, Fig. 19) developed by ARKKI was published, specifically addressing primary school teachers. It also consists of sturdy large task cards, which are delivered in a high-quality house-shaped cardboard case and are based on the curriculum of the community school. The tasks are subdivided accordingly for grades 1-2, 2-3, and 5-6. They describe the contents, tasks, objectives, and methods as well as the required materials and amount of time needed to complete assignments.

In addition, they explain how the corresponding topic touches upon different subjects and learning contents when used as a trans-disciplinary task. According to Pihla Meskanen, the publication *Tilat, talot & kaupungit*, which is also available online and can be downloaded,[48] is specifically designed for class teachers of the first six years of community school. The first six grades are interesting for the reason that interdisciplinary teaching can be realized particularly easily, because teachers for grades 1-6 teach all the subjects, and they are able to plan their own schedule and engage in multidisciplinary phenomenon-based projects.[49]

Conclusion: Baukultur-Teaching, further education and training

Germany could learn a lot from Finland at various levels. Although architecture education in Finland is not yet systematically anchored at universities and in teacher training, as explicitly called for in the 1998 *Architectural Policy* and in the 2001 report *Discovering Architecture,* it is interesting to note the ways in which architects and other planners and designers are enabled to become teachers in the school system and can therefore develop their own didactics for architecture education. A comparable Master's program for lateral entrants, such as the "q master berlin" offered by the Berlin University of the Arts, is considerably narrower in terms of admission restrictions and is aimed exclusively at candidates with a degree in fine arts, since architecture in Germany is not, as is the case in Finland, on an equal footing with the other arts.[50] In Germany, the threshold for architects and graduates of other fields focusing on planning and design who wish to change to a teaching profession is high, as they would have to complete a full teacher training program.

Germany can therefore also learn from Finnish institutions and actors to initiate smart projects that have a wide reach and require few resources, rely on peer learning, and, in the final step, even generate the requisite teaching materials—an idea that has not yet found widespread acceptance in Germany. As the network meetings of the Federal Foundation of Baukultur have shown, the field of players in Baukultur education currently consists of numerous lone warriors who compete with each other rather than being encouraged to cooperate, which may also result from the difficult funding situation. It would be desirable for Baukultur education in Germany to be orchestrated so that a central contact point can be established in order to pool forces. The report *Discovering Architecture* from 2001 shows that the situation in Finland 20 years ago was doubtlessly roughly comparable to the situation in Germany today but has changed significantly since Archinfo Finland was founded.[51] The Netzwerk Baukulturelle Bildung (Network for Baukultur Education), which was founded in 2017 by the Federal Foundation of Baukultur, and which recently gained visibility through a new internet platform,[52] certainly represents a promising initial signal. However, in order to really advance Baukultur education in Germany, there is a need for key stakeholders who develop overarching concepts, design advanced training opportunities, and actively promote, inform, and communicate visibility in the federal states and municipalities as well as in schools, public policy, and the wider political sphere.

In order to promote Baukultur education in Germany, concepts and strategies such as those developed by the Museum of Finnish Architecture or the Alvar Aalto Foundation are also needed as these are designed to break down barriers and show that it is easy to communicate architecture. They should demonstrate that there is no need for explicit expertise or a specific educational venue to introduce children and young people to architecture, but that it can happen anywhere and at any time. Teaching strategies that sensitize children and young people to everyday architecture on a low-threshold basis, such as Anke Leitzken's *Stadtsache App*, or the *SpielRaumStadt* concept and the *Stadtdenker* strategy, which were both developed in the context of experimental seminars at the University of the Arts, are currently still rare phenomena in Germany.[53] What German professionals can also learn from Finnish actors is that mediation projects require a certain sensory input in order to appear less daunting. The toolkit *Tilat, talot & kaupungit*, published *by ARKKI in* 2013, starts out from a similar point as *Curriculare Bausteine* (Curricular Building Blocks), brought out by the Wüstenrot Stiftung in 2010. They are supposed to show at which points in the German school system opportunities arise in the individual subjects and class levels to integrate Baukultur education. Similar to its Finnish counterpart, which is of course not designed as a complete program and only covers the first six grades, the German publication also provides concrete suggestions, formulates tasks, and makes these available to teachers. In their plain appearance as charts, the *Curriculare Bausteine*, however useful they may be in terms of content, seem difficult to understand intuitively and are thus almost counterproductive.[54] The Finnish toolkit's design, on the other hand, conveys a certain sensuality and playful character, which is without question suitable for breaking down inhibitions. The task cards are clearly structured and provide information on how they can be used for particular grades and which content can be combined with other subjects. Jaana Räsänen summed up the principle behind *Tilat, talot & kaupungit* when she said: "It is part of our policy to offer teachers something that is easily accessible, because they would otherwise not use it!"[55]

1 Cf. Architectural Policy 1999, p. 16.
2 Pihla Meskanen in conversation with the author, May 9, 2019.
3 Martti Raevaara in Skype conversation, June 6, 2019.
4 Pirkko Pohjakallio-Koskinen's article "Mapping Environmental Education Approaches in Finnish Art Education" describes the development of environmental education within arts classes from the 1970s to 2010. Cf. Pohjakallio-Koskinen 2010.
5 Martti Raevaara in Skype conversation, June 6, 2019.
6 Martti Raevaara in Skype conversation, June 6, 2019.
7 There is no shortage of teachers in Finland, unlike in Germany, as this is a highly respected and popular profession. On the contrary, in an interview on June 6, 2019, Raevaara feared that there could be a surplus of teachers in the coming years due to the recent serious slump in birth rates in Finland. In 2018, he reported, only 47,600 children were born—normally between 58,000 and 60,000 children are enrolled in school. Such a decline in births of 10,000 per year would mean that in six years there would be 500 class teachers too many if this trend continues. Cf. also: https://www.dfg-ev.de/news/5860 (last accessed January 7, 2019).
8 Martti Raevaara in Skype conversation, June 6, 2019.
9 Korpelainen and Yanar 2001, p. 42.
10 Jaana Räsänen in conversation with the author, June 9, 2019.
11 Pihla Meskanen in conversation with the author, June 9, 2019.
12 Jaana Räsänen via email, November 27, 2019.
13 Lotta Leskelä in phone conversation, August 30, 2019 and via email, January 14, 2020.
14 Riikka Mäkikoskela in conversation with the author, May 13, 2019.
15 Mervi Eskelinen in Skype conversation, June 6, 2019.
16 Cf. https://www.arkkiinternational.com/franchising/ (last accessed January 7, 2020).
17 Mikko Hartikainen, Jaana Räsänen, Pihla Meskanen, Mari Koskinen, and Tiina Valpola in conversation with the author, May 2019.
18 Jaana Räsänen via email, December 14, 2019.
19 Cf. Häro 1980; Korpelainen and Yanar 2001, p. 10.
20 Cf. Korpelainen and Yanar 2001.
21 Cf. Korpelainen, Kaukonen and Räsänen 2004; cf. Räsänen 2007.
22 Cf. Hänninen 2007.
23 Cf. Kataikko 2006, p. 38; cf. http://archinfo.fi/2014/01/kehitysaskel-eita-1980-2014/ (last accessed December 20, 2019).
24 Jaana Räsänen via email, January 15, 2020.
25 Lotta Leskelä via email, January 15, 2020.
26 Cf. Isohauta 2006, p. 87.
27 Cf. Kataikko 2006, p. 41; cf. Playce website: https://www.playce.org/index.php?page=main (last accessed December 20, 2019).
28 Pihla Meskanen in conversation with the author, May 9, 2019.
29 Cf. http://arkki.net/creating-the-future/ (last accessed January 7, 2020).
30 Cf. http://www.mfa.fi/ginger-bread-city (last accessed December 15, 2019).
31 Arja-Liisa Kaasinen in conversation with the author, May 9, 2019; cf. http://www.mfa.fi/lapset (last accessed December 15, 2019).
32 Arja-Liisa Kaasinen in conversation with the author, May 9, 2019 and cf. Museum of Finnish Architecture, school task set.
33 Cf. Museum of Finnish Architecture, Opetuspaketti kuvallinen katsaus suomen arkkitehtuurinhistoriaan opettaja, p. 2.

34 Museum of Finnish Architecture, "Ten Keys", p. 3.
35 Museum of Finnish Architecture, "Ten Keys", p. 9.
36 Museum of Finnish Architecture, "Ten Keys", p. 13.
37 Lotta Leskelä in phone conversation, August 30, 2019.
38 Cf. Räsänen 2006, p. 14.
39 Cf. https://www.alvaraalto.fi/en/information/aalto-cities/ (last accessed January 7, 2020).
40 Lotta Leskelä in phone conversation, August 30, 2019.
41 Lotta Leskelä in phone conversation, August 30, 2019.
42 Cf. http://archinfo.fi/2019/11/arkkitehtuurikerhot-2016-2019-hanke-nosti-arkkitehtuurikas vatuksen-saavutettavuutta-valtakunnallisesti/ (last accessed January 07, 2020).
43 Cf. Kivioja 2018, p. 5.
44 Cf. http://archinfo.fi/2016/08/eilen-tanaan-huomenna-hanke/ (last accessed December 28, 2019).
45 Cf. http://archinfo.fi/2018/01/meidan-paikka-2018/ and http://archinfo.fi/2016/08/eilen-tanaan-huomenna-hanke/ (last accessed December 28, 2019).
46 Cf. Korpelainen, Kaukonen and Räsänen 2004; cf. Räsänen 2007.
47 Cf. http://www.playce.org/uploads/pdf/Toolkit_english_lowres.pdf (last accessed January 7, 2020).
48 Cf. http://www.arkki.net/tilat_talot_kaupungit/esipuhe/ (last accessed January 07, 2020).
49 Pihla Meskanen in conversation with the author, May 9, 2019.
50 Cf. Architectural Policy 1999, p. 16; cf. Korpelainen and Yanar 2001, p. 40.
51 Cf. https://www.udk-berlin.de/fileadmin/2_dezentral/Referat_Studienangelegenheiten/UdK_Anzeiger/2019/04-2019_Anzeiger_der_UdK_Berlin.pdf (last accessed January 7, 2020).
52 Cf. Korpelainen and Yanar 2001, p. 40.
53 Cf. https://www.bundesstiftung-baukultur.de/netzwerk/bildung?bildung_bkb=All (last accessed January 7, 2020).
54 Cf. Wüstenrot Stiftung 2010.
55 Jaana Räsänen in conversation with the author, May 9, 2019.

Architectural policy programs as promoters of architecture education for children and youth in Finland

Jaana Räsänen (guest contributor)

The roots of architecture education as it is taught today can be traced to the discussion around the significance of arts education, engendered by the 1970s school reforms in Finland. Concerns around the gradually weakened position of arts and crafts subjects in schools led to the birth of an entirely new type of school system—the establishment of specific schools for visual arts.[1] Architecture education started to take small but firm steps forward when architects joined the ranks of the defenders of arts education at the end of the decade and, at the same time, produced teaching material for environmental education that had hitherto been considered too nature-oriented.[2]

In the 1990s, the act regulating the education provided by visual arts schools—devised in the 1980s—came into force,[3] the first *National Core Curriculum* was published, and, alongside art schools, three architecture schools for children and young people were established: ARKKI in Helsinki, Lastu in Lapinlahti, and Erkkeri in Turku. The first two are still operating. In addition, architecture was introduced as a long-term program in one of the visual arts schools in Jyväskylä and as various short courses in many others. It also gained an increasingly visible position in the museums of the sector. However, this was still only accessible to a select few.

The national Architectural Policy encourages discussion of architecture in schools

In 1998, the Finnish *Architectural Policy* approved by the Prime Minister's Office set the aim of reinforcing the position of architecture education in general education. According to the foreword written by the prime minister Paavo Lipponen (1995–2003): "The architectural policy emphasizes both the citizens' right and duty to take responsibility for their own environments. This is why architecture education and information about architecture needs to be enhanced."[4]

The national policy states that understanding architecture is an aspect of civic skills. Thus, studying architecture should be within the reach of everybody, especially at primary, secondary, and upper secondary schools. As one of the actions to be taken for promoting civic education in architecture the program suggests that:

"The National Board of Education strengthens the position of architectural education when creating the bases for the curriculums. In addition, the needs of architectural education are taken into consideration in the execution of the program for linking schools and the wider cultural setting."[5] Furthermore the program notes: "The key to understanding architecture lies primarily in education in the arts, and also environmental studies encompassing matters of the built environment. The improvement of the citizens' competence to participate in the decision-making concerning matters of their own surroundings will be greatly enhanced when architecture becomes part of the curriculums of the environmental studies and biology, geography or history and political sciences."[6]

According to the program, it is possible to improve popular participation in debates and decision-making processes regarding the environment by raising public awareness of architecture. This viewpoint was shared and supported by the renewed Land Use and Building Act issued in 1999.

Municipal and regional policies as messengers around the country

The first municipal and regional architectural policies were created shortly after the national one. How do they respond to the national programs initiative on promoting architecture education for children and young people?

The first wave of local policies was launched by the province of Eastern Finland in 2000 and followed by the policies of the cities of Jyväskylä and Oulu in 2002. Strengthening the status of architecture education in the local school curricula and developing architecture education as part of liberal adult education were identified as essential means of influencing the quality of Eastern Finland's built environment.[7] Jyväskylä was the first city to publish its own local policy. As measures to be taken it listed the drafting of a development program for architecture education, the mapping of individuals or bodies with expert knowledge operating in the field, and the creation of a network supporting the development of architecture education. The Alvar Aalto Museum was identified as the key conductor of this development.[8] The city of Oulu suggested an increase in environmental awareness-raising activities for children and young people in kindergartens, schools, youth clubs, courses, and summer camps.[9]

The second wave of local policies peaked in 2006 when the province of South-West Finland and the cities of Helsinki, Tampere, and Vantaa published their programs. They were followed by the cities of Lappeenranta and Kuopio in 2007, the regions of Häme in 2007 and Uusimaa in 2009, and finally the cities of Turku and Lohja in 2009, as well as the city of Lahti and the updated and officially published program of Helsinki in 2010.

The region of Satakunta started the third wave of the local architectural policies in 2013. It agreed with the previous policies by setting aims and measures to promote architecture education. Satakunta was followed by the policies of the region of Uusimaa in 2014, the second-round policies of the cities of Vantaa in 2015 and Kuopio in 2017, and finally the policy of the municipality of Kirkkonummi in 2017 and the second round of polices of Jyväskylä in 2019. At the time, architecture education was already an acknowledged field of education and recognized as a means of engendering a better understanding of the built environment and the development of participatory skills. The latest policies took this as their starting point. Rather than stipulating measures of architecture education, they instead utilized those methods and involved both children and adults in the process of creating local architectural policies.

The architectural policy of Lahti plainly states that the city will take on the responsibility of developing architecture education.[10] The other municipal and regional policies of the 2000s and 2010s recognized six main development themes for architecture education:

NETWORKING

+ using the existing networks and creating new ones for developing architecture education[11]
+ generating cooperation between different fields of expertise; locally, nationally, and internationally[12]

ARCHITECTURE IN SCHOOLS

+ strengthening the status of architecture education at all school levels from kindergartens to upper secondary schools[13]
+ discussing architecture not just in art and environmental education classes but also adapting it to various other school subjects[14]
+ involving local architects and city planners by having them visit schools[15]
+ identifying potential schools specializing in architecture[16]

TEACHING MATERIAL

+ mapping and utilizing existing teaching material, informing others about it, and developing new material[17]
+ publishing maps and guides presenting the local architecture and using the built environment as educational material[18]

ARCHITECTURE AS HOBBY

+ developing architecture education as an after-school activity at visual arts schools, youth clubs, summer courses and camps, etc.[19]
+ starting architecture education within the system of Basic Education in the Arts[20]

PARTICIPATORY SKILLS

+ developing the skills of interaction and participation and offering children and young people opportunities to effect changes in their own environment[21]

TEACHER TRAINING

+ updating the training of teachers and thus encouraging future teachers to implement architecture and environmental education in schools[22]

The impact of architectural policies of the 2000s on architecture education

When comparing the aims and measures presented by the first two waves of architectural policies to what has actually occurred in the field of architecture education, it seems obvious that these policies have had an impact.

A report based on a nationwide survey in 2000 showcased 200 initiatives across the country in which architecture education was provided within formal education as well as in the activities of diverse non-profit organizations.[23] This was followed by a period of active networking. A domestic network, Arkas, and an international network, Playce, were established and continued the discussion. After actors in the field of children's culture published their own policy program in 2003, a network of 20 (31 in 2019) children's cultural centers arose around the country, aiming to enhance the implementation of culture for all children. In this network, the field of architecture is represented by Lastu, which developed from a local player to a regional children's culture center.[24] The most recent entity to take responsibility for developing architecture education is the network of Alvar Aalto Cities.[25]

The position of architecture education in schools was strengthened when an obligatory architecture course "Environment, place, and space"[26] was introduced in the visual arts curriculum of upper secondary schools in 2003, followed by the compulsory course "Environmental aesthetics, architecture, and design"[27] for comprehensive school classes 1–7 in 2004. Those themes integrating the contents and aims of school subjects such as "Responsibility for the Environment, Wellbeing and Sustainable Future" also created opportunities for focusing on architecture during schools' project weeks. The *National Core Curriculum for Basic Education* was renewed in 2016. The first impression was that the position of architecture education had been weakened since the new curriculum did not introduce any obligatory courses and not even an explicit mention of architecture. From the end of 2019, however, the new curriculum encourages the use of varied types of environments as learning environments, and also compels schools to arrange at least part of their teaching as multidisciplinary modules.[28] This is being viewed as an inspiring opportunity to integrate architecture into different school subjects. A new phase of development has begun.

The Finnish Association of Architects SAFA answered the need for new teaching material by rolling out an architecture education website in 2005, followed by two guidebooks for architecture education. The first one explored architecture on different levels of the environment,[29] while the second guidebook introduced basic concepts of architecture.[30] In the following, the different actors such as ARKKI and Lastu—and today particularly the Museum of Finnish Architecture and the Alvar Aalto Museum—have produced pedagogical material for general use.

Ever since the national *Architectural Policy* and the 1999 Land Use and Building Act called on citizens to participate in decision-making processes concerning their own environments, architecture education has been recognized as an important resource for acquiring the necessary knowledge and skills needed for participation in the architectural realm. Most of the players in the field of architecture education have contributed to the development of participatory methods and processes. The national and regional arts councils and other public funders have actively supported this development by launching and financing numerous projects and by establishing positions for regional artists dedicated to promoting both architecture education and participatory processes.

The new *National Core Curriculum of Basic Education* has changed the work of teachers and launched a process of renewal with respect to teacher education at universities. Hopefully, architecture and built environments will be afforded sufficient attention in this process. Until now, teachers have gained most of their knowledge and experience from complementary and optional studies arranged by different organizations in the field of education and culture.

Conclusion

The power of the national *Architectural Policy* rests on the prime minister's words—which have been referenced not only in regional and municipal architectural policies but in numerous other policies, strategies, lectures, and papers as well as discussions and debates. Through all these measures, the message concerning the importance of architecture education has spread to different levels and fields of society. The power of all local policies is based on the process of engagement by means of which they are conceived. The people involved have been eager, enthusiastic, and devoted to striving for and achieving the agreed aims. Decision-makers have become aware of architecture education and its potential. Through the years, the municipalities, cities, and regions have asked architecture educators to talk about their work and have inspired local architects and art educators to venture into this realm.

Certainly, the parallel developments of architectural policies and architecture education have mutually reinforced each other's impact. Fulfilling the aims of these policies has been easy to achieve in regions and municipalities that have already featured significant players in architecture education. Over time, architectural policy programs have increased the credibility of architecture education: where it was not yet well known, it is now taken more seriously.

Today more than ever, we need to discuss the meaning of architecture, as well as how to build a sustainable future—and this message must be heard at all levels of society. Architecture education and architectural policy work can contribute to this.

1 Heinimaa 2007.
2 Härö 1980.
3 Cf. Laki taiteen perusopetuksesta 1998.
4 Cf. Architectural Policy 1999, p. 3.
5 Cf. Architectural Policy 1999, p. 16.
6 Cf. Architectural Policy 1999, p. 16.
7 Itä-Suomi (Eastern Finland) 2002, p. 19.
8 Jyväskylä 2002, p. 16.
9 Oulu 2002, p. 20.
10 Lahti 2010, p. 10.
11 Jyväskylä 2002, p. 16, Tampere 2006, pp. 28–29, Turku 2009, pp. 20–21, Lohja 2009, pp. 22–23.
12 Varsinais-Suomi (South-West Finland) 2006, p. 20.
13 Itä-Suomi (Eastern Finland) 2002, p. 19, Oulu 2002, p. 20, Tampere 2006, pp. 28–29, Helsinki 2006, p. 42, Helsinki 2010, p. 131, Kuopio 2007, pp. 20–21, Häme 2007, p. 30, Turku 2009, p. 20, Satakunta 2013, pp. 58, 63, Lappeenranta 2007, pp. 17, 25, Varsinais-Suomi (South-West Finland) 2006, p. 20.
14 Tampere 2006, pp. 28–29, Lohja 2009, pp. 22–23, Uusimaa 2014–2020, pp. 18, 40, Kirkkonummi 2017, pp. 61–62.
15 Lohja 2009, pp. 22–23, Kirkkonummi 2017, pp. 61–62.
16 Helsinki 2010, p. 131, Turku 2009, pp. 20–21.
17 Tampere 2006, pp. 28–29, Häme 2007, p. 30, Satakunta 2013, pp. 58, 63, Kirkkonummi 2017.
18 Häme 2007, p. 30.
19 Oulu 2002, p. 20, Varsinais-Suomi (South-West Finland) 2006, p. 20, Häme 2007, p. 30.
20 Varsinais-Suomi (South-West Finland) 2006, p. 20.
21 Vantaa 2006, pp. 19–20, Lohja 2009, pp. 22–23, Uusimaa 2014–2020, pp. 18, 40, Kirkkonummi 2017.
22 Kuopio 2007, pp. 20–21, Satakunta 2013, pp. 58, 63.
23 Korpelainen and Yanar 2001, p. 7.
24 Cf. https://www.lastenkulttuuri.fi/en/centres/map/ (accessed January 8, 2020).
25 Cf. https://www.alvaraalto.fi/palvelut/arkkitehtuuri-ja-muotoilukasvatus-2/alvar-aalto-kaupunkien-kouluyhteistyo/ (accessed January 8, 2020).
26 Cf. Lukiokoulutuksen opetussuunnitelman perusteet 2003, pp. 201–202.
27 Cf. Perusopetuksen opetussuunnitelman perusteet 2004, pp. 236–40.
28 Cf. Perusopetuksen opetussuunnitelman perusteet 2014, pp. 26–33.
29 Korpelainen et al. 2004.
30 Räsänen 2010.

Closing remarks

This study has undoubtedly confirmed that Finland fully deserves its pioneering status in the field of architectural policy or architecture education. However, it has also become clear that this success is the result of years of intensive and continuous work, which was by no means completed with the publication of the *Architectural Policy* in 1998 but only really began afterwards. Fears that Finland's historical and structural conditions might be so different and its advance so significant that it would be pointless to try to learn from the country have proved unfounded. The starting conditions for cultivating interest in Baukultur and, ultimately, basic public knowledge are certainly somewhat more favorable in Finland, given its particular history and the importance of architecture in the context of its nation-building experiences. However, the challenges facing architecture-mediating institutions and their actors in Finland are hardly different from those in Germany. They have merely begun earlier and are therefore currently operating with greater confidence and in a more self-evidently public manner. In Germany it is not even certain whether and how this work may be taken up seriously, as a corresponding funding policy is currently still lacking. In both nations, architectural policy is a cross-sectoral task in which as many stakeholders and positions as possible must be involved and in which duties and responsibilities must be clearly identified and assigned.

It has become clear that this process is by no means easier in a small country like Finland than it is elsewhere. Inter-ministerial cooperation is a challenge everywhere and the search for partners and allies requires time and patience.

With regard to the question of integrating architecture education into the school system, it has become apparent that, from a purely formal point of view, the conditions in Germany are perhaps somewhat better than in Finland. Surprisingly, more arts lessons are provided for in the local curricula, and architecture has already been consistently included in German curricula, at least within the subject area of art. However, the example also illustrates that it is not enough to write architecture into the curricula, but that active work is needed to ensure that teachers are able to work on this topic with pupils. The example of Finland shows that it is first of all necessary to create an awareness of architecture education and its potential as a cross-cutting and transferable task between the most diverse school subjects but also between the individual arts. As the example of many Finnish schools shows, if this awareness is encouraged it is also possible to use the guidelines of the curricula creatively.

The only real advantage that Finland has actually had—and which probably cannot be overestimated for the development and implementation of the *Architectural Policy*—is the fact that, from the very beginning, there has been strong support for it at the highest political level. Paavo Lipponen, who was prime minister from 1995 to 2003, made the *Architectural Policy* his personal concern, as Tiina Valpola noted in conversation with the author. In an interview he gave to the magazine *Arkkitehti-lehti* in 2005 in his capacity as speaker of parliament, he made the following statement on the subject: "Finland needs active architectural policy if it wants to be seen as a leading country in architecture also in the future. It would be of prime importance to assemble for the implementation of architectural policy sufficient economic and political resources and to regard the further development of this policy as a permanent aspect of our administrative culture."[1] And Lipponen's successor, Matti Vanhanen, prime minister from 2003 to 2010, also gave a clear statement in the article: "In view of our own welfare and standard of living, we as a nation cannot afford a poorer standard of building than past generations. ... Each street corner and city block must be a unique place to be recognized and of which we can be proud."[2]

Although Baukultur in Germany has now also arrived at the political level—thanks to the Federal Foundation of Baukultur that was established in 2007—there is no substantial support for it. On the contrary, it can be assumed that Baukultur is likely to face similar difficulties in the political as in the public sphere. Seen in this light, it seems more than reasonable that Germany should primarily follow the model of the old *Architectural Policy* of 1998. Like Finland at that time, Germany now needs a declaration of principles, which first define the value and significance of architecture in general terms at the cultural, sociological, and economic levels. Furthermore, public authorities should be encouraged to act as role models. An orientation towards Finland's first architectural policy program also seems reasonable because it can be assumed that, in terms of architecture education, Germany may be at the point Finland was 20 or 25 years ago. This can be seen, for example, in *Discovering Architecture. Civic Education in Architecture in Finland*, a report published by SAFA in 2001. The chapter "Challenges and Needs" could be left virtually unchanged to describe the current challenges and demands for Baukultur education in Germany.[3] As the report shows, countless projects in the field of architecture education had already been funded during the first enthusiastic wave of implementation of the *Architectural Policy* in Finland. In contrast, the funding situation in Germany is still completely unresolved and certainly poses the greatest challenge.

While one can only hope that the German *Guidelines for Baukultur* will become more than just a cultural proclamation, the new Finnish architectural policy program APOLI 2020 can be looked forward to with anticipation, as it is to be expected that the new position paper will also set international standards and possibly bring about innovations in the field of architecture education as well. The latest headlines from Finland indicate that a new phase of architecture and design education has just begun. On December 12, 2019, it was announced that the New Museum of Architecture and Design, which is currently in the planning stage, has received a grant of 450,000 euros from the Finnish Cultural Foundation in order to establish a "Centre for Architectural and Design Learning." According to the design museum's press release, the aim is to create a center that brings together and interacts with different players, operating as a kind of "logistics center" or "distribution point" that brings knowledge and expertise to wherever it is needed. The four-year project will develop the learning center, organize a nationwide educational tour, and design and implement a nationwide training program. The result will be a completely new type of public relations work which will represent a new way of thinking about the museum, and where the various activities will be taken out of the traditional museum context. Accordingly, the initial plan is to develop the Centre for Architecture and Design Learning into an "immaterial center of learning," information exchange, and networking that is not bound to a physical location. If possible, however, it should later be given physical space within the New Museum of Architecture and Design.[4]

1 Hautajärvi 2005, p. 20.
2 Hautajärvi 2005, p. 21.
3 Cf. Korpelainen and Yanar 2001, pp. 40–42
4 Cf. https://www.designmuseum.fi/fi/events/suomen-kulttuurirahasto-myonsi-designmuseon-ja-arkkitehtuurimuseon-yhteishankkeelle-450-000-euron-uuruisen-apurahan-uuden-arkkitehtuurin-ja-muotoilun-oppimisen-keskuksen-luomiseen/ (accessed January 19, 2020).

The *German Guidelines for Baukultur* should essentially contain a declaration of principles, which should first of all define the value and significance of architecture in general terms at the cultural, sociological, and economic level. It would be advisable to lay the foundations for recognizing architecture and Baukultur as a central component of art and culture.

The guidelines should be understood as the public authorities' self-declaration to act as role models. They should declare the improvement of architectural awareness in society as a central goal, and Baukultur education should consequently play a more prominent role.

It would seem sensible to formulate the *Guidelines for Baukultur* with as much openness as possible and to address them to the federal states and municipalities as an explicit invitation to take action, so that they can become more concrete from one level to the next. The municipalities can then directly negotiate what issues affect their citizens.

* * *

The process of establishing these guidelines should be organized in such a way that at the federal, state, and local level, the most comprehensive network of players possible is involved in the planning process, since Baukultur is a cross-disciplinary issue that affects almost all social areas.

The more departments, institutions, associations, and actors are involved in the process, the more likely it is that they will later show a willingness to actively participate in and support the implementation.

In order to be able to actively involve as many parties as possible in the process, it is advisable, as was done in Finland, to present the results of the working group to a wider circle of actors for comment.

The example of Finland shows that it makes sense to clearly define responsibilities in the guidelines and address them accordingly.

* * *

The adoption of the German *Guidelines for Baukultur* should not be seen as the end of the process but rather as the actual beginning, which initiates a cooperation between ministries, actors, and interest groups from politics and civil society.

Finland's experiences have shown that it would be useful to evaluate the process at regular intervals—roughly every three or four years—and to thereby subject the guidelines to regular revision. This will ensure that the process of creating these guidelines remains a vital learning process.

There is a need for constant contact partners and individual people in charge who are dedicated to the topic in order to support a continuous implementation process and the further development of the guidelines, to carry out public relations work in the federal states, regions, or municipalities, and to provide advice and assistance in the development and revision of local guidelines. In Finland, the post of special advisor for architecture (2004–2012) was established before Archinfo Finland provided technical support for the process.

* * *

In order to improve the awareness of Baukultur in society *in the long term*, the German *Guidelines for Baukultur* should recommend that Baukultur education is integrated more systematically into the educational system. The most efficient and democratic way would be to integrate architecture education into the school system, which is already an intention formulated in German curricula.

To ensure that teachers are able to meet the requirements, Baukultur education should be integrated into teacher training seminars at universities and pedagogical colleges, and especially into artistic teacher training. It would also be reasonable to set a course for creating a professional science within the field of Baukultur education, with the aim of developing not only specialist didactics based on practical research but also to create new teaching materials and advanced training concepts.

In order to enhance Baukultur awareness in society in the *short term*, the German *Guidelines for Baukultur* should recommend the development of advanced education and training programs to support teachers in integrating Baukultur education into the school system. It would be desirable for architecture and Baukultur to be experienced as cross-disciplinary subjects that are predetermined for a multidisciplinary way of teaching.

In order to be able to act swiftly and on a broad front, it would, as a first step, make sense to offer already active parties advanced training opportunities, which would enable them to expand their range of subjects pedagogically, methodologically, and in terms of content. In addition, they should be supplied with methods and strategies that enable them to turn the accompanying teachers into multipliers while working with children and young people, so that these teachers can carry out projects independently or with minimal assistance in the following years. In this way, Baukultur education would spread exponentially and quite rapidly so that it could be integrated into school practice much more efficiently.

In order to make teaching materials available promptly, it could be useful to acquire licenses for successful Finnish concepts and toolkits and then adapt these to the German market.

* * *

It would be advisable to integrate Baukultur education into adult education and thereby promote its introduction at adult education centers and private art schools.

Ideally, schools of architecture for children and young people should be promoted and established according to the Finnish model, such as the "Baukasten Bremen."

* * *

The German *Guidelines for Baukultur* should promote low-threshold access and approaches that fundamentally sensitize people to architecture and Baukultur and do not primarily focus on the outstanding and special. Instead of normative quality criteria, Baukultur should be defined with more openness, as has already been done in the "Leipzig Charta" (2007) or the "Davos Declaration" (2018).

* * *

Essential for the future of Baukultur education is, however, the provision of subsidies to finance projects, concepts, advanced training courses, teaching materials, and higher-level coordination efforts. In order to anchor Baukultur education in society, the mediation must be taken out of voluntary work and a way must be paved for the increasing professionalization of Baukultur mediators.

In order to be able to anchor Baukultur education more firmly in society, there is a need for reliable and consistently available contact persons and individuals in charge, who are dedicated to the topic and have the necessary resources and backing to be able to offer support, inform, mediate, plan advanced training events, or build bridges to other institutions in the sector. The Finnish example demonstrates that there is no urgent need for institutions with a large number of staff to succeed in conveying Baukultur (or that provide support at the level of architectural policy), but that it is possible to achieve a great deal as an immaterial institution with a limited number of people but with smart strategies designed to make use of existing resources and with the impetus and wherewithal to establish lasting cooperation across a wide variety of sectors and fields.

References

Archijeunes, ed. *Baukulturelle Bildung an Schweizer Schulen.* 2019. https://www.archijeunes.ch/article/studie-baukulturelle-bildung-an-schweizer-schulen-download/ (accessed October 10, 2019).

Arts Council of Finland and Ministry of Education, ed. *The Finnish Architectural Policy. The Government's architectural policy programme 17 December 1998.* 1999. http://archinfo.fi/wp-content/uploads/2014/02/SAKSA.pdf (accessed August 15, 2019).

Bundesstiftung Baukultur. *Dokumentation des Konvents der Baukultur 2018, Forum 2.* 2018. https://www.bundesstiftung-baukultur.de/sites/default/files/medien/81/downloads/konvent2018_forum2_baukulturelle_bildung_dokumentation_1.pdf (accessed October 10, 2019).

Busnach, Zlil. *Arts Education in Finland.* Utrecht 2017. https://www.lkca.nl/~/media/downloads/bijeenkomsten/dutch-scandinavian%20exchange/finland.pdf (accessed January 6, 2020).

Competition Program. *National Museum Annex "New National".* 2018. https://www.uusikansallinen.fi/wp-content/uploads/2019/01/LIITE-A3-kilpailuohjelma-englanti-teksti-kaaviokuvat-.pdf (accessed January 19, 2020).

Curtis, William. *Architektur im 20. Jahrhundert.* Stuttgart: DVA, 1989.

Detlefs, Beate. "Oodi – eine Ode an Finnlands Bibliotheken." *BuB Forum Bibliothek und Information.* 14.02.2018, https://b-u-b.de/oodi/ (accessed September 15, 2019).

Feller, Barbara. *Architektur- / Baukulturvermittlung für junge Menschen. Zur Situation in Österreich.* Wien 2009. https://architekturstiftung.at/nachrichtenstudie-architektur-baukulturvermittlung-fuer-junge-menschen/studie-architektur-baukulturvermittlung-fuer-junge-menschen (accessed December 15, 2019).

Fröbe, Turit, ed. *Stadtdenker. Ein Spielraum für urbane Entdeckungen.* Berlin: Jovis, 2014.

Fröbe, Turit and Winderlich, Kirsten, eds. *SpielRaumStadt. Baukulturvermittlung für Kinder.* Oberhausen: Athena Verlag, 2017.

Fröbe, Turit. *Alles nur Fassade? Das Bestimmungsbuch für moderne Architektur.* Köln: DuMont, 2018.

Griffiths, Gareth. *The Polemical Aalto.* Tampere: Datutop, 1997.

Hänninen, Anna. *Matkalla arkkitehtuurin maahan* (On the way to the land of architecture). 2007. https://docplayer.fi/2841951-Matkalla-arkkitehtuurin-maahan.html (accessed December 20, 2019).

Härö, Merja. *Viihtyisä ympäristö: Ympäristökasvatuksen virikekirja.* (Agreeable environment: A book of environmental education) Suomen arkkitehtiliitto SAFA, 1980.

Hartikainen, Mikko. "Art and Architecture Education in Finland." In *Creating the Future,* edited by ARKKI, 6–9. Helsinki 2009. http://arkki.net/creatingthefuture/wp-content/uploads/2019/03/Art-and-Architecture-Education-in-Finland_Creatingthefuture1.pdf (accessed January 19, 2020).

Hautajärvim, Harri. "What is the significance of architecture? Questions to the Speaker of the Finnish parliament and the Prime Minister." *Arkkitehti-lehti* 2/2005, 20–21.

Heinimaa, Elisse. *From art school to basic education of art.* 2007. https://youngart.fi/in-english/from-art-school-to-basic-education-of-art/ (accessed January 22, 2020).

Hietala, Anu. *In-school and out-of school arts education in Finland.* LKCA conference in Utrecht, The Association of the Basic Education in the Arts, 26.01.2017. https://www.lkca.nl/~/media/downloads/bijeenkomsten/dutch-scandinavian%20exchange/ppt%20finland%20anu%20hietala.pdf (accessed January 22, 2020).

Hubrich, Hannes. "Baukultur in der Ausbildung von Pädagogen. Architekturseminare für zukünftige Kunsterzieher, Architekten, Gestalter und Künstler an der Bauhaus-Universität Weimar." In *Kinder_Sichten: Städtebau und Architektur für und mit Kindern und Jugendlichen,* Edelhoff, Silke, Kataikko, Päivi and Uttke, Angela, eds., 84–93. Troisdorf: Bildungsverlag EINS, 2006a.

Hubrich, Hannes. "Citizen Education as Part of Architectural Studies: an official 'Architecture and Children'-course at the Bauhaus University Weimar." In *Playce. Architecture Education for Children and Young People,* Laaksoonen, Esa and Räsänen, Jaana, eds., 77–82. Helsinki, 2006b.

Kanerva, Anna and Mitchell, Ritva. *Compendium of Cultural Policies and Trends in Europe. Country Profile Finland.* Helsinki 2017. https://www.culturalpolicies.net/wp-content/uploads/pdf_full/finland/finland_032017.pdf (accessed January 22, 2020).

Kataikko, Päivi. "Baukultur als Bürgerbildung – das Beispiel Finnland." In *Kinder_Sichten. Städtebau und Architektur für und mit Kindern und Jugendlichen,* Edelhoff, Silke, Kataikko, Päivi and Uttke, Angela, eds., 36–41. Troisdorf: Bildungsverlag EINS, 2006a.

Kivioja, Johanna and Räsänen, Jaana, eds. *Salvos. Architectural education in Youth Art Schools carrying out Basic Education in the Arts.* 2018

Korpelainen, Heini, Kaukonen, Hille and Räsänen, Jaana. *Arkkitehtuurin ABC: Löytöretki rakennettuun ympäristöön* (Architectural ABC: Discovering the built environment). 2004. https://drive.google.com/file/d/0BwYhOKq9ezGuVXlwTmRGLXFUb0U/view (accessed December 20, 2019).

Korpelainen, Heini and Yanar, Anu. *Discovering Architecture. Civic Education in Architecture in Finland. Report.* Helsinki 2001.

Leitzken, Anke M. and Lachmuth, Anne. *Entdecke Deine Stadt.* Weinheim/Basel: Beltz & Gelberg, 2017a.

Leitzken, Anke M. and Lachmuth, Anne. *Jetzt entdecke ich meine Stadt.* Weinheim/Basel: Beltz & Gelberg, 2017b.

Leitzken, Anke M. *Stadtsache APP.* 2018. https://www.stadtsache.de/ (accessed September 20, 2019).

Meskanen, Pihla. *Architecture Education – Initiating a Change!* SchulRaumKultur Symposium. Linz, 2012. http://2012.schulraumkultur.at/assets/papers/meskanen-architecture-education-initiating-change.pdf (accessed January 22, 2020).

Meyer, Ulf. *Architekturführer Helsinki. Bauten und Projekte von 2017.* Berlin: DOM Publishers, 2018.

New National Competition Program. https://www.uusikansallinen.fi/wp-content/uploads/2019/01/LIITE-A3-kilpailuohjelma-englanti-teksti-kaaviokuvat-.pdf (accessed January 17, 2020).

Nikula, Riitta. "Die Zeit zwischen den Weltkriegen: Die Architektur der jungen Republik." In *Finnland: Architektur im 20. Jahrhundert,* Stiller, Adolf, ed., 50–97. Salzburg/München: Verlag Anton Pustet, 2000.

Pohjakallio-Koskinen, Pirkko. (2010): "Mapping Environmental Education Approaches in Finnish Art Education." In *SYNNYT/ORIGINS,* No. 2, 2010: 67–76.

Rambow, Riklef. *Experten-Laien-Kommunikation in der Architektur.* Münster/New York/München/Berlin: Waxmann, 2000.

Räsänen, Jaana. "Architecture Education in Finland." In *Playce. Architecture Education for Children and Young People*, Laaksoonen, Esa and Räsänen, Jaana, eds., 13–18. Helsinki, 2006b.

Räsänen, Jaana. *Arkkitehtuurin ABC 2: Peruskäsitteitä* (Architecture ABC 2: Basic Concepts). 2010. https://drive.google.com/file/d/0BwYhOKq9ezGu-VXlwTmRGLXFUb0U/view (accessed January 19, 2020).

Räsänen, Jaana, ed. *The ABC of Architecture, Basic Concepts*. Finnish Association of Architects. 2014

Rauterberg, Hanno. "Architektur als Volkssport." *Die ZEIT*, 41/2000, Hamburg October 5, 2000. https://www.zeit.de/2000/41/200041_conradi.xml (accessed August 15, 2019).

Salmela, Marja. *Tulevaisuuden suomea Rakentamassa. Arkkitehtuuripolitiikan uudistamisen suuntaviivoja* (Building the future of Finland. Guidelines for the architectural policy reform). 2017. https://api.hankeikkuna.fi/asiakirjat/96d04b34-fa2a-495c-890c-04a51f6d3c-b7/511639ea-f102-4b7b-9862-443d140824c3/RAPORTTI_20190506093914.pdf (accessed January 19, 2020).

Salokorpi, Asko. *Finnische Architektur*. Frankfurt/M, Berlin, Wien: Ullstein, 1970

Tuormala, Petri. "Architectural Policy Programmes in Finland – Perspectives on Local Level." In *Nordic Journal of Architectural Research*. No. 1. 2017: 85–110. http://arkitekturforskning.net/na/article/viewFile/965/905 (accessed January 19, 2020).

Valpola, Tiina. *Elaboration and Realization of Architectural Policies on National and Municipal Levels*. Unpublished presentation as part of the EFAP conference, November 18-20, 2011, Gdańsk.

Valpola, Tiina. *Architectural policies for regions and cities*. Luxembourg 12. November 2015. http://archinfo.fi/wp-content/uploads/2016/09/LUX12.11.2015.pdf (accessed January 22, 2020).

Wäre, Ritva. "Von der historischen Architektur zur frühen Moderne." In *Finnland: Architektur im 20. Jahrhundert*, Stiller, Adolf, ed., 16–49. Salzburg/München: Verlag Anton Pustet, 2000.

Working Group on the Follow-up to the Architectural Policy Program, 2002, *Valtioneuvoston arkkitehtuuripoliittisen ohjelman toteutumisen seuranta ja jatkotoimenpiteet*. http://julkaisut.valtioneuvosto.fi/bitstream/handle/10024/80836/opmtr28.pdf?sequence=1&isAllowed=y (accessed January 19, 2020).

Wüstenrot Stiftung. *Bildungsorte und Lernwelten der Baukultur. Momente und Prozesse baukultureller Bildung von Kindern und Jugendlichen*. 2019.

Zetterberg, Seppo. "Finnland – historischer Überblick." In *Finnland: Architektur im 20. Jahrhundert*, Stiller, Adolf, ed., 10–15. Salzburg/München: Verlag Anton Pustet, 2000.

Acts, National Core Curricula etc.

Finnish National Agency for Education, ed. *National Core Curriculum for Basic Education 2014*. Helsinki, 2016.

Finnish National Agency for Education, ed. *National Core Curriculum for General Upper Secondary Schools 2015*. Helsinki, 2016.

Finnish National Agency for Education, ed. *National Core Curriculum for the general and advanced syllabi for Basic Education in the Arts 2017*. Helsinki 2018.

Laki taiteen perusopetuksesta (424/1992) and Laki taiteen perusopetuksesta (633/1998) (Basic Education Act), https://www.finlex.fi/fi/laki/ajantasa/1998/19980633 (accessed January 15, 2020).

Land Use and Building Act (132/1999, Finlex). https://www.finlex.fi/en/laki/kaannokset/1999/en19990132 (accessed January 15, 2020).
Lastenkulttuuripoliittinen ohjelma. Opetusministeriön julkaisuja 2003:29. (Children's Cultural Policy Program), http://urn.fi/URN:ISBN 952-442-542-4 (accessed January 15, 2020).
Lukiokoulutuksen opetussuunnitelman perusteet 2003. (National Core Curriculum Upper Secondary Schools). https://www.oph.fi/sites/default/files/documents/47345_lukion_opetussuunnitelman_perusteet_2003.pdf (accessed January 15, 2020).
Perusopetuksen opetussuunnitelman perusteet 2004. (National Core Curriculum Basic Education 2004). https://www.oph.fi/sites/default/files/documents/perusopetuksen-opetussuunnitelman-perusteet_2004.pdf (accessed January 15, 2020).
Perusopetuksen opetussuunnitelman perusteet 2014. (National Core Curriculum Basic Education 2014). https://www.oph.fi/sites/default/files/documents/perusopetuksen_opetussuunnitelman_perusteet_2014.pdf (accessed January 15, 2020).

Local and regional architectural policy programs in Finland

Architectural Policy Program for the Province of Eastern Finland, 20.11.2000: http://archinfo.fi/wp-content/uploads/2014/02/Apoli-Ita-Suomi.pdf (accessed January 15, 2020).
Architectural Policy Program of Jyväskylä, 17.6.2002: http://archinfo.fi/wp-content/uploads/2014/01/Apoli-Jyvaskyla-FI.pdf (accessed January 15, 2020).
Architectural Policy Program of Oulu, 29.10.2002: http://archinfo.fi/wp-content/uploads/2014/01/Apoli-Oulu.pdf (accessed January 15, 2020).
Architectural Policy Program of Southwest Finland, 2006: http://archinfo.fi/wp-content/uploads/2014/02/Apoli-Varsinais-Suomi.pdf (accessed January 15, 2020).
Architectural Policy Program of Vantaa, 2006: http://archinfo.fi/wp content/uploads/2014/02/Apoli-Vantaa.pdf (accessed January 15, 2020).
Architectural Policy Program of Tampere, 2006: http://archinfo.fi/wp-content/uploads/2014/02/Apoli-TampereFI.pdf (accessed January 15, 2020).
Architectural Policy Program of Helsinki, 2006: http://archinfo.fi/wp-content/uploads/2014/02/Apoli_Helsinki1.pdf (accessed January 15, 2020).
Architectural Policy Program of Häme, 2007: http://archinfo.fi/wp-content/uploads/2014/02/Apoli_Häme.pdf (accessed January 15, 2020).
Architectural Policy Program of Lappeenranta, 29.10.2007: http://archinfo.fi/wp-content/uploads/2014/02/Apoli-Lappeenranta-FI.pdf (accessed January 15, 2020).
Architectural Policy Program of Kuopio, 2007: http://archinfo.fi/wp-content/uploads/2014/02/Apoli_Kuopio.pdf (accessed January 15, 2020).
The architectural policy program of Uusimaa and Eastern Uusimaa, 2009: http://archinfo.fi/wp-content/uploads/2014/02/Apoli_Uusimaa.pdf (accessed January 15, 2020).
Architectural Policy Program of Turku, 16.2.2009: http://archinfo.fi/wp-content/uploads/2014/02/Apoli_Turku_pdf_2_.pdf (accessed January 15, 2020).
Architectural Policy Program of Lohja, 2009: http://archinfo.fi/wp-content/uploads/2014/02/Apoli_Lohja.pdf (accessed January 15, 2020).
Architectural Policy Program of Lahti, 2010: http://archinfo.fi/wp-content/uploads/2014/02/Apoli_Lahti.pdf (accessed January 15, 2020).
Second Architectural Policy Program of Helsinki, 2010: http://archinfo.fi/

wp-content/uploads/2014/02/APOLI2010_internet.pdf (accessed January 15, 2020).

Architectural Policy Program of Satakunta, 2013: http://archinfo.fi/wp-content/uploads/2014/02/Apoli_Satakunta.pdf (accessed January 15, 2020).

Second Architectural Policy Program of the Region of Uusimaa, 2014–2020: https://www.uudenmaanliitto.fi/files/15240/Yhteinen_metropolimme_Arkkitehtuuripoliittiset_tavoitteet_2014-2020.pdf (accessed January 15, 2020).

Second Architectural Policy Program of Vantaa, 2015: https://www.vantaa.fi/instancedata/prime_product_julkaisu/vantaa/embeds/vantaawwwstructure/126289_Vantaan_arkkitehtuuriohjelma_2015.pdf (accessed January 15, 2020).

Architectural Policy Program of Kirkkonummi, 2017: https://www.kirkkonummi.fi/library/files/5b235e08c91058630b000df3/A-poli__kunnanvaltuuston_14.5.2018_hyv_ksym_.pdf (accessed January 15, 2020).

Second Architectural Policy Program of Koupio, 2017: https://www.kuopio.fi/documents/7369547/7450879/Apoli_250x210_FINAL_web.pdf/00136840-82ff-493f-a8e4-c559a522b-c0d (accessed January 15, 2020).

Second Architectural Policy Program of Jyväskylä, 2019: https://www.jyvaskyla.fi/kaavoitus/projek-tit-ja-ohjelmat/avoin-kaupunkiym-paristo (accessed January 15, 2020).

Image credits

Fig. 1
Helsinki Central Railway Station by Eliel Saarinen (1904–19), © Turit Fröbe

Fig. 2
Enso Gutzeit Company Headquarters, Alvar Aalto (1962), © Wikimedia Commons/CC BY-SA

Fig. 3
Finlandia Hall Helsinki, Alvar Aalto (1971), © Garett Wollman/Wikimedia Commons/CC BY-SA

Fig. 4
Lifeguard tower Aurinkolahti Beach in Vuosaari, © Turit Fröbe

Fig. 5
Retro-architecture in Berlin, © Turit Fröbe

Fig. 6
"Lasipalasti" in Helsinki by Viljo Revell, Heimo Riihimäki und Niilo Kokko (1936), © Wikimedia Commons/CC BY-SA

Fig. 7
Amos Rex by JKMM Architects (2018), © Turit Fröbe

Fig. 8
Oodi by ALA Architects (2018), © Kuvio

Fig. 9
Oodi "Book Heaven", © Kuvio

Fig. 10
Oodi, "Livingroom", © Risto Rimppi

Fig. 11
Dummy of the Berlin Bauakademie (2004–2019), © Turit Fröbe

Fig. 12
Arabic translation of the Finnish Architectural Policy, 2007, © Arts Council of Finland and Ministry of Education. Drawing: © The National Board of Antiquities; Photo: © MW/ Maija Kairamo

Fig. 13
Schematic representation of the first two implementation phases of Finnish Architecture Policy, © Tiina Valpola

Fig. 14
Helsinki Architectural Highlights, Archinfo (2017), © Inka Saini/Finnish Association of Architects SAFA

Fig. 15
Screenshot of the Audience Favorites, Mai 15, 2019, © www.uusikansallinen.fi/ The National Museum of Finland

Fig. 16
Screenshot of the Finalists, September 26, 2019, © www.uusikansallinen.fi/The National Museum of Finland

Fig. 17
First place "Atlas" by JKMM Architects, © JKMM Architects

Fig. 18
Kuopio: Distribution of classroom hours: Basic education 2019, © https://www.slideshare.net/jukkasormunen/presentation-of-educational-structure-in-kuopio-and-finland-education-system-242019 (accessed January 7, 2020)

Fig. 19
Toolkit "Tilat, talot & kaupungit" (2013) by ARKKI, © Turit Fröbe

Imprint

Supported by:

Federal Ministry
of the Interior, Building
and Community

Federal Institute for
Research on Building,
Urban Affairs and
Spatial Development

within the Federal Office for
Building and Regional Planning

Universität der Künste Berlin

grund_schule der künste

Cover:
Mini-Tapiola in Tapiola (Espoo),
© Turit Fröbe

Translation:
Dominique Haensell and Mieke Woelky

Design and typesetting:
Simon Steinberger

Typefaces:
High Life (Dinamo),
Neue Haas Unica (Linotype)

Lithography:
Bild1Druck, Berlin

Printed in the European Union

Bibliographic information published by the Deutsche Nationalbibliothek
The Deutsche Nationalbibliothek lists this publication in the Deutsche Nationalbibliografie; detailed bibliographic data are available on the Internet at http://dnb.d-nb.de

jovis Verlag GmbH
Kurfürstenstraße 15/16
10785 Berlin
www.jovis.de

jovis books are available worldwide in select bookstores. Please contact your nearest bookseller or visit www.jovis.de for information concerning your local distribution.

ISBN 978-3-86859-616-8